Who Cares?!
The Unique Teaching of
Ramesh S. Balsekar

Also by Ramesh S. Balsekar

The Happening of A Guru (2003)
Confusion No More (2003)
Guru Pournirma (2003)
Peace and Harmony in Daily Living (2003)
The Ultimate Understanding (2001)
Advaita, the Buddha and the Unbroken Whole (2000)
It So Happened That. The Unique Teaching
    of Ramesh S. Balsekar (2000)
Sin and Guilt: Monstrosity of Mind (2000)
Meaningful Trivialities from the Source (2000)
The Infamous Ego (1999)
Who Cares?! (1999)
The Essence of the Bhagavad Gita (1999)
Your Head in the Tiger's Mouth (1997)
Consciousness Writes (1996)
A Net of JeweLs (1996)
The Bhagavad Gita - A Selection (1995)
Like a Large Immovable Rock (1994)
Ripples (1994)
Consciousness Speaks (1992)
From Consciousness to Consciousness (1989)
The Final Truth (1989)
A Duet of One (1989)
Experiencing the Teaching (1988)
Explorations into the Eternal (1987)
Experience of Immortality (1984)
Pointers from Nisargadatta Maharaj (1982)

Who Cares?!
The Unique Teaching of
Ramesh S. Balsekar

Edited by
Blayne Bardo

Advaita Press

Copyright © 1999 by Ramesh S. Balsekar

First Published in India by

ZEN PUBLICATIONS

5 Raja Bahadur Building, 156 J. Dadajee Road, Tardeo,
Mumbai 400 034. India. Tel.: (91 22) 492 2429, 491 8258.
Fax: (91 22) 492 2429. E-mail: zenlinks@vsnl.com

Published in the USA by

Advaita Press
PO Box 3479
Redondo Beach, CA 90277
Tel: 310-376-9636
Email: fellowship@advaita.org
www.advaita.org

Credits:
Cover Design : Chetna Bhatt

ISBN: 0-929448-18-9
Library of Congress Catalog Card Number: 99-62314

Dedicated to Nisargadatta Maharaj

Contents

Acknowledgements

Nothing happens but that it was to happen—the supposed individuals are merely characters within that event, any event. There is no one to give credit to or any thing to take credit for—by the same token there is no question of any blame, nor of any failure. (LR 9)

Truly, Guru and disciple are a single movement in Consciousness, and in the fullness of this understanding there arises inexpressible appreciation and gratitude for all that has been given through you. Dear Ramesh, thank you.

ৰৰৰ

There are three primary reasons I am grateful for having been asked to compile and edit a second book for the Guru. First, it is something I can give to Ramesh. Second, it is yet another gift to provide a wider audience with access to the teaching as it happens through Ramesh. And third, I have the opportunity, which I missed the first time, to thank Sharda, Ramesh's wife. Thank you Sharda Maaji for your kind and gentle concern, silent and expressed support, and the relaxing and insightful conversations over coffee and tea.

Any polished book, especially one compiled and edited in a short span of time, is the result of devoted proofreaders and readers catching errors and contributing their suggestions. My heart-felt appreciation goes out to each of you: Susan Herbert, Jennifer Claire Moyer, Faye Fields, Chaitan Balsekar, Gerry Hackman, Mark Worthington, and Avinash Kadam.

Due to the thoughtfulness and generosity of Ben Pierce, privately published and valuable substance for the book magically appeared at my door via courier. Other key materials were provided by Kanwarjit Singh, satsang tapes, and by Jennifer Claire Moyer and Giovanna Dalle Rive Carli, several transcriptions.

So many kind and generous people contributed to my being able to live in Bombay while working on the book—Luzius Jegher, Catherine M. Asche, Ben Pierce, Philippe and Geraldine de Henning, Narayani Etienne, Claudia Nangoi, Gert Seglitz, and David and Faye Fields. Warm thanks to each of you.

Thank you, Bianca, for a beautiful cover!

The book was gratefully produced on two computers: the first, a generous loan from Rajiv M. Naik, and the second, a state-of-the-art rental spontaneously and magnanimously provided by William Van Braam.

And at the last moment in a flurry of energetic generosity and hospitality, Madhukar Thompson donated staff and equipment for laser printing the pages of the book for the press.

Introduction

The unique teaching happening through Ramesh is pure Advaita.

Why pure? Because the *entire* teaching is unequivocally a single concept—*Consciousness is all there is*. It is not two, the meaning of *a + dvaita*. There is *not* the manifestation and all of its objects *plus* Consciousness, or whatever name you call That which cannot be named. *All there is is Consciousness.* There is no ego deciding to do spiritual seeking. If this were the case, then there would be *two*—Consciousness and ego. There is *only* One without a second. Pure Advaita. *Consciousness is all there is!*

Why unique? Because Advaita has never been presented precisely the way the teaching *happens* through Ramesh. Ramesh repeatedly points out that whatever he says is not the Truth—"Anything any sage or any scripture has ever said is a *concept* and consequently can be either agreed or disagreed with." His teaching is unique because he tells the seeker *not* to try to remember what has been taught—"In every effort to remember, the ego is present. The ego is absent only when the *understanding* brings about the *remembering*." There is uniqueness because he says, "Accept the ego! Resisting the ego only nourishes it." And there is uniqueness in that Ramesh begins with bhakti, or devotion, and ends with jnana, or final understanding—"... accepting that 'I' am nothing, that 'I' am merely an object at the will of God is basically nothing but pure devotion, or bhakti. So what I say strictly begins with bhakti: Thy will be done." Finally, if there is intent listening or reading, then there will be no doubt as to the *exact* teaching happening through Ramesh.

The importance of this last point is easily missed. Ask yourself the same question that Ramesh often asks seekers attending satsang for the first time: "What is the understanding now?" In other words, as a result of all the seeking, whether having had teachers or reading books, what *exactly* is the understanding that you, the reader or listener, has right now? Very few can say!

After sitting in five or six satsangs you realize that the entire teaching as it happens through Ramesh is precisely stated in five words—Consciousness is all there is. Or if you wish, All there is is Consciousness. That's it! If these five words are spontaneously and totally intuited in the heart, then the process of seeking has ended and the final event has happened. If not, then more concepts are given, and the teaching unfolds simply.

For "whom"? That's the point. *Seeking* comes for the teaching in the form of "seekers" believing that "they" are purposefully seeking something. For these seekers the teaching is conceptually developed. In other words, the primary concept of Consciousness is all there is, is explained the only way which is possible—with further concepts.

The second basic concept of the teaching is—there is no doer. All which happens is the impersonal functioning of Consciousness, or God's will. With this, the teaching is then developed:

The apparent manifestation is a reflection—which is simultaneously both real and unreal—of Consciousness within Itself. Human beings are body-mind organisms—objects having no free will. Ego is the sense of doership, not just the identification with name and form, which is created by Divine hypnosis for life to happen as we know it. Spiritual seeking may happen if it is the destiny of the body-mind organism and the will of the Source. If it does, it begins with an ego and, if it is destiny, ends in the annihilation of the ego. Consciousness is all there is!

The working concept for Who Cares?! was four-fold: to clearly present the teaching as it happens through Ramesh with minimum interference and maximum input from him; to accomplish this by quoting from recent satsangs and Ramesh's other published works; to make it as seeker friendly as possible—there is a glossary of concepts and all quotes from published works are noted; to keep the completed work half as long as either *Consciousness Speaks* or *Your Head In The Tiger's Mouth*; and to have the final manuscript carefully read and approved by Ramesh. Accomplishing these, everything would be in one place, easily accessible, authentic, and portable.

ༀༀༀ

The glossary contains brief definitions of all the major concepts used in the teaching. For example, if there is any confusion over the meaning Ramesh gives to the related concepts of destiny, programming, and conditioning or to the concepts of duality and dualism—the glossary quickly provides the clarification.

However, there are four words which frequently occur throughout the presentation of the teaching, the significance of which is often not appreciated. Except for one, they are not typically part of the spiritual or philosophical vocabulary. Because of one's casual familiarity with these words, the pivotal and deep meaning they have in the teaching may escape attention.

> *God* - This word or concept is frequently used by Ramesh to indicate or refer to That which cannot be conceived and thus is beyond mind-intellect. God is not an object or an entity and has no qualities. That which is beyond mind and consequently cannot be conceived is *referred to* as God or any number of references such as Consciousness, Source, Noumenon, I-I, Reality, Tao, Potential, Subject, Absolute, Primal En-

ergy, or whichever concept. The teaching as it happens through Ramesh is not theistic. (In theism God is an object and an entity with qualities such as omnipresence, omniscience, all merciful, etc.)

happens - This indicates an occurrence without any doer doing anything. "Happens" is spontaneous and without intention or volition, although there usually appears to be a chain of events, cause and effect, which leads to something that *just happens*. The meaning of this word is best conveyed by two examples:

- "The teaching *happens* through Ramesh." In other words, there is no "one" who does anything. It, the teaching, *happens*.
- "There is no seeker. The seeking is just *happening*."

arises - This has the same meaning in the teaching as "happens."

functioning - Consciousness is all there is. There is no doer, no seeker, no decision maker, no lover, *but* there is *doing, seeking, deciding, loving*. "Functioning" is the impersonal movement of Consciousness-in-action that gives the manifestation the *appearance of being real*. For example, the ego, sense of personal doership, interprets as "its functioning" that which is always and can only be the impersonal functioning of Consciousness through a body-mind organism.

ৰৰৰ

In a recent satsang Ramesh was asked how he explained the increase in the number of seekers all over the world, the apparent "quickening" of realization happening in body-mind organisms, the ever increasing number of books and magazines devoted to the subject, *and yet* he was known for his quoting Lord Krishna in the *Bhagavad Gita* about how few seekers there are. Ramesh's response:

> It simply means there are more people so there are more seekers. "Out of thousands there is one seeker, and among seekers hardly one knows Me in principle." That is what Lord Krishna says. So there are more people and there are more seekers. If there are more seekers there are more Gurus, and if there are more Gurus there are more books!

ৠৠৠ

If this apparent editor were granted one heart-wish in the totality of the impersonal functioning of Consciousness, it would be that all spiritual seekers arrive at the attitude of "who cares?" thus setting the stage in the process of seeking for the final, total understanding to *happen*. And that it happens! But who is there to care?

Manifestation
an apparent tapestry
ever being woven spontaneously
in the Present Moment
with a single thread—
Consciousness

At the feet of the Guru,

Blayne Bardo
Bombay
March 1999

Who Cares?!

Every month the disciple faithfully sent his Master an account of his progress.

In the first month he wrote: "I feel an expansion of consciousness and experience my oneness with the universe." The Master glanced at the note and threw it away.

The following month, this is what he had to say: "I have finally discovered that the Divine is present in all things." The Master seemed disappointed.

The third month the disciple's words enthusiastically exclaimed: "The mystery of the One and the many have been revealed to my wondering gaze." The Master shook his head and again threw the letter away.

The next letter said: "No one is born, no one lives, and no one dies, for the ego-self is not." The Master threw his hands up in utter despair.

After that a month passed by, then two, then five months— and finally a whole year without another letter. The Master thought it was time to remind his disciple of his duty to keep him informed of his spiritual progress.

Then the disciple wrote back: "Who cares?"

When the Master read those words a look of great satisfaction spread over his face.

1

A Seeker Hearing the Teaching
for the First Time

RAMESH A seeker hearing the teaching for the first time is often stunned, even if the seeking has been going on for twenty years.

ཨཨཨ

RAMESH People are told by masters that they should fight the ego, kill the ego, but what I'm saying is to *accept* the ego. Is that not unique? Don't fight the ego. Accept the ego. Why, because "you" didn't create the ego. The Source has created the ego, and the Source is in the process of destroying the ego in some cases. That's why your head is in the tiger's mouth. There's no escape. There is no escape if you fight the ego. That's my point. If you keep on fighting the ego, the tiger will have its mouth open for ages and ages. You accept the ego, and the tiger will snap its jaws quickly.

Forget the Teaching

RAMESH This teaching in many ways is unique. Usually with a teaching, it is to make a note of it, study hard, use it in practice. What I'm telling you is, *forget the teaching*. Let it work by itself. Very important!

Forget the teaching because "who" wants to remember the teaching? It's the *ego* that wants to remember the teaching and wants to use that teaching to achieve something. But if you forget the teaching, then the teaching leading to the understanding will work by itself. And if the teaching doesn't lead to the understanding, then it's not worth it. So either way, forget the teaching! It's either effective or not effective. If it's not effective then there's no question. If it is effective, let it be effective!

Will the ego want to contribute to its own annihilation? No. The ego wants the teaching *only* to be able to use it, to achieve something—not for its own annihilation. If the teaching is forgotten the ego is forgotten, and the teaching works by itself.

Your effort is the obstruction. That's why I say forget the teaching—don't try to use it. Let that understanding work at whatever level.

Bhakti Begins the Teaching

RAMESH   People ask me if there is anything unique about what I am saying. I'd say yes. What is unique about what I am saying is that I begin with bhakti and end in understanding. What is bhakti? Thy will be done. The "me" says "You are all there is—Thy will be done."

WARRICK   *When you say "Thy will be done," I understand you to mean that God's will is, in fact, always being done.*

RAMESH   That is correct. Was *being* done, is *being* done, and will *be* done!

WARRICK   *And it is impossible for anything but God's will to be done.*

RAMESH   That is correct. But, truly, that is not the relevant part. The relevant part is, *"I" am nothing*. That is the relevant part. You [God] are all there is. Your will prevails all the time. Therefore to think, "I can do anything; I can do something; I can achieve something" is ridiculous. That is the relevant part—the helplessness of a created object. Acceptance, total acceptance of the fact a created object is helpless, is the relevant part.

Whose will prevails—and you call that God—is a concept which is necessary because the individual finds himself or herself so helpless. So the mind-intellect creates an object which is all-powerful and then says everything happens according to Thy will—which means it is not "my" will. So accepting that "I" am nothing, that "I" am merely an object at the will of God is basically nothing but pure devotion, or bhakti. So what I say strictly begins with bhakti—Thy will be done.

Basic Teaching

[Frequently visitors are asked by Ramesh to relate the process of their seeking. And one question he often asks is: "What is your basic understanding now, as a result of the teachers you've studied with and the books you've read?" Not once, as far as I know, has anyone been able to say *precisely* what his or her basic spiritual understanding is. Whether one agrees or disagrees with Ramesh is not the point, but the visitor has no doubt as to Ramesh's description of the fundamental teaching.]

RAMESH   Do I have a basic? Yes. My basic is Consciousness is all there is—no "one" *does* any action. Nothing happens unless it is God's will. And when I say "God," I don't mean an all-powerful entity within or outside of the manifestation. By "God" I mean the Source, Consciousness—the One without the second—reflected within which the functioning of the manifestation happens.

The Buddha said, "Events happen. Deeds are done. There is no individual doer thereof." That's the basic. No one could have put it in briefer or simpler terms. Events *happen*. Deeds are done. There is no individual doer thereof. If there is no individual doer, then "who" does it is irrelevant. But if the intellect asks the question and must have an answer, then the intellect is told, "Whose action? God's action."

No One Speaking and No One Listening

ARTHUR *Why does Ramesh keep speaking?*

RAMESH Oh, Arthur! Ramesh doesn't speak. Nor, really, does Arthur listen. There is no Ramesh to speak and there is no Arthur to listen. But so long as there is an "Arthur" to listen, Arthur needs concepts. Consciousness provides those concepts through this body-mind organism.

ARTHUR *So I was wondering why Ramesh keeps speaking to Arthur.*

RAMESH Because that is part of the functioning of manifestation. That is part of *What-Is* at the moment. *That* is what is supposed to happen, and it happens! Nothing can happen unless it is supposed to happen. So this conversation is happening. What effect this conversation has on whom, nobody knows—only Consciousness, God, knows.

VIMAR *For me concepts are concepts. I have come across many mythologies from different masters, and they are good stories.*

RAMESH Yes! They are stories! So what you are asking is how do you know that what I'm saying is the truth. That's your question, isn't it?

VIMAR *Exactly!*

RAMESH I've just given you the answer. *Nobody* can tell you the Truth. Whatever anybody tells you is a concept.

VIMAR *What is beyond the concepts?*

RAMESH Beyond the concepts is Truth! The Truth is hidden by concepts and conceptualizing.

Silence and a Simile

RAMESH When you talk and use a simile, the simile is based only on objects. Therefore, as Ramana Maharshi often said, "The only teaching is silence." You use any concept, you use any simile, you use any metaphor—all are based on objects.

TIM *Is there transmission of knowledge through silence?*

RAMESH Is there transmission of the Truth through silence? Yes. But very, very, very few organisms are programmed to be able to accept the Truth through silence. Therefore, out of compassion for the many, many who are not programmed to be able to accept the Truth through silence, Ramana Maharshi started to talk. He used a simile as an example to explain this: some few are like gunpowder, one spark and it goes. Seekers who are like gunpowder may not be able to accept the silence but one spark, one statement—All there is is Consciousness, no "one" does anything, nothing happens unless it is the will of God— and the gunpowder is annihilated. So who is programmed to be the gunpowder, who is programmed to be the dry coal, and who is programmed to be the wet coal is God's will. But to the wet coal which needs a lot of work, Ramana Maharshi again gave some consolation—your head is already in the tiger's mouth, there is no escape. So let it take as many births as the Source wants.

Life Has No Value

ALTA *Why was all this initiated in the first place?*

RAMESH You paint a picture with a figure in it, and the figure wants to know why you painted the picture. The only answer is that you felt like it.

You see, you take a child to the seashore, give it a spade and a bucket. Promptly it will begin digging sand and piling it up into a castle or a mountain. It will take a lot of trouble over it for some time. But when the parent says it's time to go home, the child will kick down the castle over which it had spent a lot of trouble building. If you ask the child, "Why did you take the trouble to build it and now you have destroyed it?" the child will not understand your question. But if you insist he will say, "I built the castle because I liked to build it. I destroyed the castle because I liked to destroy it."

The whole point is that the mind-intellect, which is ego, is conditioned from the beginning that everything must have a purpose. Life must have a purpose. Why, because life is precious. All you have to do is watch the TV, *National Geographic* or the BBC channel. You watch *Nature* and you see that life is anything but precious. Life has no value. Don't you feel it? It has no value. A bird lays eggs, and another one eats them, and then something else eats it.

Find out if life really has any meaning or whether life is precious. It just happens. *It just happens*. The mind-intellect gives meaning and *then* wants to know the meaning. Life has no meaning. The real meaning of life is that *life has no meaning*. It just *happens*.

The Meanest

PHILIPPE *After meeting some of the upcoming Advaita teachers, I really appreciate the way you formulate things. You're the meanest of all. You're the one who puts it right there immediately with great honesty. I think we all appreciate that very much.*

RAMESH You mean I'm the meanest of the lot because I don't hold out carrots. I'm saying there are no carrots to have. Most people would like to have some carrots offered. Those people who still want carrots will go to the place where they will get carrots, and having eaten the carrots, they'll find themselves still dissatisfied and will come here.

Clarity or Confusion

PREM *Ramesh, I also love to hear you. Somehow you have such a unique clarity of description.*

RAMESH Did you say unique? How? The Truth is only One.

PREM *The Truth is One, but it seems that every expression is unique, and although somehow the results are the same ...*

RAMESH The result is either confusion or clarity. Every teacher is unique, producing either confusion or clarity. So if a teaching produces confusion, why does it? The teacher certainly didn't intend that you should be confused.

PREM *Maybe the teachers themselves are confused, therefore...*

RAMESH Now, why are the teachers confused? Because it is God's will.

PREM *Yes, of course!*

RAMESH Why are the teachers confused? Because they

should confuse others. And why does this happen? Because it is God's will. Do you know why it is God's will? There is a verse in the *Bhagavad Gita* which says: "There is only one seeker among thousands of people, and among those who seek hardly one knows me in principle." So the thousands of seekers have got to be confused. How can they be confused unless there are teachers who are confused? Even that is God's will—that is my point.

PRATIMA   *Or the teacher may not be confused, but the disciple isn't ready.*

RAMESH   Sure. Then that is God's will.

PRATIMA   *So we can't blame the poor teachers totally.*

RAMESH   You can't blame *anybody* for *anything*. That is why it is also said in the *Bhagavad Gita*: "You can commit no sin nor can you do a meritorious deed. Your original understanding is clouded by ignorance. That is why you think in terms of sin and merit." This is what Lord Krishna says in the early part of the *Gita* and ends up: "Surrender to Me and I will save you from all sins that you cannot help think you are doing." That you think you cannot not commit sins is also God's will. So if you think you are committing sins, "surrender to Me" and I'll relieve you of all sins. Surrender. But the joke is even the surrendering is not in your control. Why? Because so long as there is an individual who says "I surrender," there is a surrenderer—there is an individual ego.

PRATIMA   *That's reassuring, the* Bhagavad Gita *having the contrast there. It's saying this on one hand and then later saying the other. This is very beautiful that there is a place for everything.*

RAMESH   Why does Lord Krishna say, "I'll save you from sins," because he knows that Arjuna's understanding, which is based on the programming of that body-mind organism, prevents Arjuna from understanding the Truth at the highest level. So Lord Krishna comes down to Arjuna's level: At your level you think that you are committing sins, then surrender to Me and I'll save you. But what I'm saying is even the *surrendering* is not in Arjuna's hands.

PRATIMA *So the contradiction there is ...*

RAMESH There is no contradiction at all. Why? The understanding is: "I can commit no sin because I commit no action. I don't do any action, how can I commit a sin?" If that understanding happens suddenly, if it is God's will, then the rest of it is not relevant. But if the body-mind organism is not programmed for the sudden understanding to happen, then Lord Krishna comes down to the lower and lower levels of the millions of Arjunas.

Divine Joke - Ego "Wanting" Annihilation

RAMESH The resistance *is* the ego, and the ego, I'm not joking, will not easily give up.

ROBERT *But the desire to have the ego annihilated is the very thing that keeps the ego alive.*

RAMESH You see, that is the joke. That is the Divine joke. The ego is Divine hypnosis. Where did the ego come from? That is the question, isn't it? Everybody says the ego is the problem. All you have to do is simply give up "your" ego. But nobody tells you how to give up "your" ego. "You" are the ego! The "me" is the ego, and the ego is not going to commit suicide. The ego could only have come from the same Source from which everything has come. The physical manifestation has come from the Source. The fictional "me" has come from the Source.

Why did the Source create the fictional "me," because without the "me" interhuman relationships would not happen. And without interhuman relationships, life as we know it could not happen. So for life as we know it to happen—for God's *lila*, or game, to happen—interhuman relationships have to happen. And for interhuman relationships to happen the ego has to be there. Ego simply means the creation of a feeling through Divine hypnosis that "I" am a doer and a separate being in control of this body. But all that really exists is the body-mind organism and the energy flowing through it.

That is the basis, exactly like there is an electrical gadget and electricity functioning through that gadget. But if the electrical gadget were hypnotized then the electrical gadget would think in terms of "*me*" producing the toast, "*me*" producing the mixture, "*me*" producing the light. Basically it is only the electricity and the gadget. Here it is only the same thing—Source, God or Energy, and the body-mind organism through which the Energy, or God, is functioning. So God has created the ego, and it is God who starts the gradual process of annihilation of the ego in some cases.

Destiny to Come and Listen

RAMESH   It is the will of God and the destiny of a body-mind organism to be able to come and listen to what is said. Even being able to listen is really and truly the grace of God. And *total* listening is also God's will and the destiny of the body-mind organism through which seeking is happening. So many people come here and they don't truly listen. While they are hearing what is said, the thinking mind is very active, ready to put up objections—"Yes, but!" and "Ah, but!" That is what the thinking mind does. So being able to listen totally is the will of God and the grace of God.

10

If you are able to listen totally, then the consequences will be quite different from listening half-heartedly and with "Yes, but!"

No "One" Can Get Enlightenment

RAMESH What is the significance of the statement, "No one can get enlightenment."? What does it mean? This is the very root of the teaching. It means that it's stupid for *any* so-called master to ask anyone to do anything to achieve or get enlightenment. The core of this simple statement means, according to my concept, that enlightenment is the *annihilation* of the "one" who "wants" enlightenment. If there is enlightenment—which can only *happen* because it is the will of God—then it means that the "one" who had earlier wanted enlightenment has been annihilated. So no "one" can achieve enlightenment, and therefore no "one" can enjoy enlightenment.

Million Dollars or Enlightenment

RAMESH   Getting enlightenment is not in your control. Getting a million dollars is also God's will and the destiny of the body-mind organism. So whether you want a million dollars or you want enlightenment and whether you get what you want are not in your control. If you think it is in your control, I suggest that you go after a million dollars instead of enlightenment, because if you get the million dollars then there will be someone to enjoy that million dollars. But if you go after enlightenment and enlightenment happens, there will be no "one" to enjoy enlightenment.

2

Consciousness Is All There Is

AUGUSTE *What is Consciousness, really?*

RAMESH Consciousness is the One without the second—
the Source of everything.

ষষষ

The "who," the "what," the "where," and the "when"
are all conceptual images in Consciousness. They are all
"real" as any mirage or dream. ... The totality of
manifestation, and everything therein, is Consciousness
Itself, the Unicity. All there is is Consciousness, not aware
of Itself in Its noumenal Subjectivity, but perceived by Itself
as phenomenal manifestation in Its objective expression. If
this is understood in depth, there is nothing more to be
understood. Why? Because such understanding must
comport the realization that there is no individual entity as
such. What we *think* we are is merely an appearance, an
insubstantial shadow, whereas what we really and truly
are, is Consciousness Itself, the formless Brahman. (FT 8)

ষষষ

All that exists is universal Consciousness. The universe
as such is not the universal Consciousness, but
Consciousness *is* the universe, just as the bracelet is made

13

of gold but the gold is not made of the bracelet. Whether the manifested universe exists or not, Consciousness is there as the subjective Absolute. ... There is no causal relationship between Consciousness and the universe. The truth is that Consciousness alone exists and is immanent in what appears as the universe. In other words, Consciousness and the universe are not two in which any sort of relationship could exist. (FT 16-17)

ৰৰৰ

The simple situation is that the appearance of the universe exists in infinite Consciousness, just as the notion of distance or emptiness exists in space. ... It is Consciousness alone that exists. It creates the illusion of the world-appearance and the ego-sense, and perceives the illusion of diversity in what is truly pure Unicity. ... It seems difficult to comprehend how the universe could exist in the infinite Consciousness that is supposed to be transcendental. Truly there is nothing other than Consciousness, and therefore Consciousness cannot but be immanent in everything that appears to exist. And yet no phenomenal manifestation can have any kind of relationship with Consciousness because a relationship can exist only between two different entities. It is in this sense that Consciousness is transcendental to the manifested universe. The universe exists in Consciousness like future waves in a calm sea—only *apparently* different in potentiality. (FT 19-20)

ৰৰৰ

What appears within Consciousness as its own reflection—the manifestation of the universe—is not separate or different from Consciousness. While the shadow, *by itself,* has no existence and is therefore unreal, the shadow is not different from the substance *when seen together.* When there is no mind in operation, when there is

14

no conceptualizing, it is clearly known, felt, experienced, that phenomenality is only the objective expression of the subjective Noumenon. ... God is that formless Subjectivity, pure Potential, the infinite, universal Consciousness which alone exists even after the cosmic dissolution. It is only within this pure, infinite Consciousness, the Potential Plenum, that phenomenal manifestation arose as a mere reflection of that Potentiality, as a mere objective expression of that pure Subjectivity. The phenomenal objectivization of this pure Subjectivity appears and functions in our *outer* world of consciousness in the waking state, precisely like sentient and insentient objects seem to exist and function in the *inner* world of consciousness in the dream state. Nothing really happens. (FT 33)

ཟཟཟ

The final truth, as Ramana Maharshi and Nisargadatta Maharaj and all the sages before them have clearly stated, is that there is neither creation nor destruction, neither birth nor death, neither destiny nor free will, neither any path nor any achievement. (FT 9)

Consciousness-at-Rest, Consciousness-in-Action, I Am

All there is is Consciousness. In that original state—call it Reality, call It Absolute, call It Nothingness—there is no reason to be aware of anything. So Consciousness-at-rest is not aware of Itself. It becomes aware of Itself only when this sudden feeling, I Am, arises. I Am is the impersonal sense of being aware. And that is when Consciousness-at-rest becomes Consciousness-in-movement, when Potential Energy becomes actual energy. They are not two. Nothing separate comes out of the Potential Energy.

Consciousness-in-movement is not separate from

Consciousness-at-rest. Consciousness-at-rest becomes Consciousness-in-movement, and that moment that science calls the Big Bang, the mystic calls the sudden arising of awareness. ... When you talk of Reality, you have converted Reality into a concept. Reality, as a word, is a concept. Reality, as Reality, is not something that you can think of. When you are the Reality, you cannot talk of Reality. So the moment you talk or think of something, it is in phenomenality and therefore conceptual. (CS 22-23)

I-I, I Am

LANCE   *I am having problems with the I-I and the I Am.*

RAMESH   There is no problem because they are not two. They are not two. Consciousness-at-rest is I-I. When It is in movement It is I Am. So I-I is a concept with which you are not really concerned. It is just a concept. What you are really concerned with is I Am.

LANCE   *I Am is the totality of manifestation.*

RAMESH   That is correct.

LANCE   *So if you are in the sleeping state, what is it then?*

RAMESH   I Am, because there is a body there and because it is in phenomenality.

LANCE   *So when there is no manifestation there is just I-I?*

RAMESH   Correct.

LANCE   *In a book about Ramana Maharshi it says that when you take the enquiry Who am I? backwards, there is nothingness.*

16

RAMESH   You see, Ramana Maharshi, therefore, does not really distinguish between I-I and I Am because it is useless. I-I is merely a concept about which he said why bother. You are only concerned with I Am and I am Lance. And when Lance is not there, I Am is there.

LANCE   *What is the dream state, then?*

RAMESH   The dream state is identified Consciousness-in-action. What is the living dream, then? The living dream is the dream of the I Am. Lance has a personal dream and I Am has the living dream. So what happens really is that you wake up from your personal dream into the living dream.

LANCE   *In deep sleep there is I-I?*

RAMESH   I Am! You are really not concerned with I-I.

LANCE   *But right now there is a need to know.*

RAMESH   Then where did I Am come from? That is a conceptual question. And for that conceptual question the conceptual answer is I Am is the activized, impersonal Energy in manifestation, and I-I is the Potential Energy. The personal "I" which Lance thinks "he" is, is the impersonal Energy identifying as an ego which thinks it is a doer and needs to know. When there truly are no more questions, then there is no doer. When there is no doer, then there is no ego. And when there is no ego, then the I Am shines forth from a body-mind organism without personal identification. When the body-mind organism dies, then the I Am continues as I Am. And when the totality of manifestation ends, then I Am is I-I, Consciousness-at-rest. And all of this is a concept. (TM 332-333)

ཨཨཨ

PETER *You said the "I" in I Am is not the ego. But what is it? I did not get it when you said the I-I.*

RAMESH   You see, Consciousness not aware of Itself, Potential Energy, is a concept. Make no mistake! I-I, I Am, I am Peter—the whole thing is a concept in order to understand your true nature. So I-I is Potential Energy before the manifestation.

PETER *The manifestation of me.*

RAMESH   No. The totality of manifestation.

PETER *So this is totally nonindividual, this I?*

RAMESH   Right. Well, actually, whether it is I-I, I Am—they are not two. I-I becomes I Am in manifestation. I-I becomes aware of Itself as I Am. But It is the same one Consciousness.

PETER *Is it a name for Consciousness? Is it a label for Consciousness?*

RAMESH   That is right. A concept. That is why I keep saying that I Am becomes a concept when you *talk* about it. This pure Awareness of Existence is the Truth, but the moment I *talk* about It, It becomes a concept.

PETER *What is the relation between Consciousness and the word "I"?*

RAMESH   It is just a name given to Consciousness.

PETER *Oh! Yes. It is just what you call a label.*

RAMESH   Yes, it is. You see, even "Consciousness" is a label. "God" is a label.

PETER   *Yes. it's confusing using the "I" that we use for our individuality in this context.*

RAMESH   Therefore I say I-I, I Am, and I am Peter.

PETER   *These are three different I's.*

RAMESH   Or it is the same Consciousness, but the relevance is to a different point.

PETER   *Yes. The last one for the ego.*

RAMESH   The last one for the ego.

PETER   *The middle one, I Am ...*

RAMESH   Impersonal Consciousness.

PETER   *And the I-I ...*

RAMESH   Is the impersonal Consciousness before ...

PETER   *Potentialization, manifestation.*

RAMESH   Yes. Quite right. Again they are words to explain something. You see?

PETER   *Yes. Yes.*

DURGANAN   *This Consciousness, or God, has no characteristics...*

RAMESH   It has no characteristics. Characteristics refer to an object, and *This* is pure Subjectivity. The Source of everything. (TM 285-286)

Concept, I Am, Present Moment

RAMESH You must have heard me say it one hundred times: whatever I say is a concept. Whatever any sage has said at any time is a concept. Whatever any scripture of any religion has said is a concept. That God is a concept and that there is no God are concepts. The only thing which is not a concept is that which no one can deny—that he or she exists—I Am, I Exist. *Impersonally* there is existence. *Personally* there is no existence.

PHILIPPE *Yes. That's tricky because that sense of existence as soon as it is captured, is a "me" again.*

RAMESH Sure. So you see, I Am is always the Present Moment. The I Am *is* the Present Moment. In the I Am there is no need for any one to say, "I Am"—because there is no one who says, "I'm not." You see? That is why it is impersonal Awareness. It is impersonal Consciousness. ... I Am is Consciousness aware of Itself. ... Then what is the Source of I Am? Consciousness *not* aware of Itself. So Consciousness not aware of Itself becomes aware of Itself as I Am. (TM 201)

ཨ ཨ ཨ

RAMESH Consciousness is all there is. When Consciousness-at-rest goes into movement, manifestation arises. The functioning of manifestation is LIFE as we know it. Nothing can *happen* in life unless it is the will of the Source, or Consciousness.

When faith in the will of God is lost—even that would be God's will!—kindness and compassion come in. When kindness and compassion are lost, there arise moral do's and don'ts. When morality is lost, religious dogmas come in. Religion being the husk and not the kernel of faith in God, religious wars begin.

3

Manifestation

RAMESH   All there is is Consciousness. That is the Source from which the manifestation has come. The functioning of manifestation is life as we know it, and in the functioning of manifestation nothing happens because it is the individual's will. *Nothing can happen unless it is the will of God,* and by "God," I mean the Source.

So first, all there is is the Source. Call it Consciousness, call it the Self, as Ramana Maharshi said, call it what you like, but understand that what is meant is the one Source— One without the second. All there is is the Source from which has come this manifestation and the manifestation is the totality of objects. The human being is a species of object with the additional, dubious gift of the sense of personal doership, which is the ego. I repeat, the human being is no more than an object, a species of object, along with all other objects that form the totality of the objects in the manifestation.

In the *functioning* of manifestation comes the second basic concept—no "one" *does* anything. Nothing *happens* unless it is the will of the Source, the will of God. This means the ego is an illusion. The sense of personal doership is an illusion. This is the final understanding.

The final understanding is that *there is no ego* as something distinct from the Source that becomes one with the Source. As long as you say "I am That," the personal

"I" is a separate one from the Source, and what I am saying is, there is no "I" at all—the "I" meaning the "me." The ego does not become one with the Source. The ego disappears into the Source when there is the *total unconditional acceptance* that there *never was the ego*.

A Reflection

RAMESH   ... where I Am is concerned, whether there is manifestation or not, makes no difference. The manifestation has come from the I Am. The functioning of the manifestation is in the I Am. It is like a reflection in the mirror. So what you accept is that whatever happens is merely a reflection in the I Am. All manifestation is a *reflection* in the Source—otherwise, there would be two.

PETER   *So it can't be a reflection of the Source, it's a reflection in the Source?*

RAMESH   It can only be *in* the Source. All this is a reflection *in* the Source because the Source is all there is. So whatever happens, you choose a concept. You can't do without concepts, otherwise you have to remain silent. And if the question "Who am I?" arises, that is the very first thought which needs an answer. The answer is a concept, a concept being something which points to the Truth. The value or usefulness of the concept is only to the extent that it points to the Truth. You see? And this concept—that the totality of manifestation and the functioning of this manifestation is a reflection in the Source—is a pointer to the Truth, *which is the Source.* (TM 21)

༄༄༄

> *"Just as the surface of a mirror exists within and without the image reflected in the mirror, so also the supreme Self exists both within and without the physical body." (19)*

Ashtavakra points out in this important verse that what we Noumenally are is definitely not a thing or an object, which the personal pronoun cannot help suggesting, but more of a process or a background, like the screen on which a movie is seen. In the absence of the background there could be no appearance at all, although in the case of the phenomenal manifestation, the "background"—Consciousness—is Itself responsible for and constitutes the appearance. The point is that unless there is total "withdrawal" into impersonality, the consideration of "who (or what) am I" may mean in effect too simple a transference from phenomenality to Noumenality. It would not have the strength to break the conditioning brought about by the notion of identity leading to the supposed bondage. It is only a direct withdrawal into impersonality that is more likely to bring about the startling transformation known as *metanoesis,* whereby there is a sudden and immediate conviction that the identification with a separate individual entity never did really exist and was essentially nothing but an illusion.

Perhaps it is for this reason that Ashtavakra suggests the mirror simile for Consciousness, which reflects everything, retains nothing, and in Itself has no perceptible existence. That is to say, Consciousness is the background of what we appear to be as phenomenal objects, and yet it is not anything objective. Just as the reflection in the mirror is a mere appearance without any existence, and the mirror is the one which has existence but is not affected in any way by the reflection, so also the psychosomatic apparatus [body-mind organism], being only an appearance in Consciousness, has no independent existence. The Consciousness in which it appears is not affected in any way by the appearance of the objects therein.

Ashtavakra in this verse brings out the transcendent aspect of the unmanifest Absolute in relation to the image or appearance of the manifest phenomena. (DO 33-34)

ཨ༠ཨ

RAMESH The Source, which has created this manifestation within Itself as a reflection, is making that manifestation function. So the manifestation and its functioning, which we call life—all of it is a reflection in the Source. ... First, there is the Source. The Source creates a reflection. The reflection is I Am. ... Now, Ramana Maharshi says the Source is the I-I. He calls It I-I merely to distinguish It from I Am. I-I is the Potential Energy. The Potential Energy activates Itself as manifestation as I Am and becomes aware of the manifestation. The I Am is the impersonal Awareness of the manifestation and its functioning. Then, for the functioning of the manifestation to occur, the Source—or God, or I Am—creates these body-mind organisms, and thus individual "me's," by identifying Itself with these body-mind organisms. So the Universal Energy, the Potential Energy, activates Itself into this manifestation. I-I on actualization becomes I Am, and I Am becomes I am Markus. Why does I Am become Markus? Because without Markus and all the billions of other names, life as we know it would not happen. (TM 28-31)

Simultaneously Both Real and Unreal

RAMESH ... Then, is the manifestation real? It is real and unreal. The question—Is the manifestation real or not?—is *misconceived*. The manifestation is both real and unreal: real to the extent that it can be observed, unreal on the basis that it has no independent existence of its own without Consciousness. So the only thing that has independent existence of its own is Reality, and that Reality is Consciousness. Consciousness is the only Reality. Everything else is a reflection of that Reality within Itself. (TM 180)

A Pot and Immanence

"Just as the all-pervading space is both inside and outside the pot, so also the eternal and all-pervading Consciousness is immanent in all beings and objects." (20)

The boundary of the pot may appear to condition and limit the space within the pot but in fact space, as such, cannot be conditioned by the pot which itself exists in space. Similarly, although the universal Consciousness may appear to be conditioned by the individual psychosomatic apparatus, all phenomenal objects are merely appearances in Consciousness. All there is is Consciousness, immanent in everything phenomenal, inasmuch as there cannot be any phenomena without Consciousness. In this concluding verse, Ashtavakra brings out the importance of emphasizing the ground—the background and the immanence—rather than the personal element so that the final spotlight is not so much on the true nature of the self but more on the withdrawal into impersonality. Instead of saying that "your" true nature is Consciousness, he says that all there is, within and without all phenomena, is Consciousness. (DO 34-35)

A Shadow and Duality

RAMESH *(Speaking with Scott)* Ramana Maharshi, as the final truth, begins by saying there is no creation and no dissolution. So if there is no creation, "who" can ask any questions? If it is accepted that there is no creation, then the creation that is seen is illusory. The basic point is this: Unicity—the Source (non-duality)—is really a concept. Manifestation (duality), also a concept, is what we live in. Thus all questions will be in duality.

If there is no creation, obviously there cannot be any Scott. But there is a Scott. So is there a Scott or is there not a Scott? The answer is *not* yes or no. The answer is yes in certain circumstances, no in other circumstances.

For example, you go out into the sun. There is a shadow. Is the shadow real or unreal? The answer is the shadow is real in certain circumstances and unreal in other circumstances. When you go out into the sun, the shadow is very much real—you can see it. But when you come inside, when you are home, there is no shadow. Likewise, when you are in duality Scott exists. But when you are not in duality—when you are in deep sleep—there is no Scott. So Scott exists in the waking state, in duality, and Scott does not exist in deep sleep.

The intellect says, "Tell me yes or no." And the answer is you cannot have a yes or no—yes in certain circumstances and no in other circumstances. The question that is asked is always in duality—when "Scott" exists. That has to be accepted. So long as "Scott" exists as the ego, the "me," there will be questions.

SCOTT *How is it that you remain firmly seeded in That? It's in and out, for me. In and out.*

RAMESH There is always a flip-flop—no questions then suddenly questions arise. Eventually, at a certain point the understanding comes on top that there is truly no "one" to ask any questions. No questions. So this flip-flop, the understanding coming up and the understanding being covered by dualism, keeps on happening until there is the final unconditional acceptance that there is truly no ego as the doer.

Duality and Dualism

The human being experiences this basic duality of the

observed object and the observing object. But along with the basic split of duality, the human being functions in dualism, which is the mental split between the "me" and the other. It is in the mind that the separation between "me" and the other arises. That is where the separation from duality to dualism occurs.

The basic split of duality happens in Consciousness Itself, as a part of the process of perceiving the manifestation. For any manifestation to exist, it has to be observed. For observing to happen an observed object and an observer object are required. This duality between the observer object and the observed object is the basic split. In the human, the split goes even deeper into the dualism of "me" and the other. The observer object assumes the subjectivity of the Absolute or Totality or God, saying, "I am the subject, the rest of the world is my object." The moment the "me" and the other come into play, duality gets further subdivided into dualism. The observer object considers himself the observer subject, the experiencer, the doer.

Enlightenment is merely the reverse process where the pseudo-subject realizes that there cannot be a separate entity and the body-mind can only function as an instrument in the manifestation of Totality. When the sense of doership is lost, dualism is restored to its basic duality. Duality is an essential mechanism in phenomenality. Enlightenment is thus nothing but the reverse process from dualism to duality, the end of the sense of personal doership. There is the deepest possible realization that the individual human being is not a separate entity, but merely an instrument through which Totality or God functions. That is all it really means, a transformation from oneself as doer to an absence of the sense of doership. (CS 111-112)

ༀༀༀ

... right and wrong, happiness and sorrow are pairs of interdependent opposites without which there cannot be any life in this world. The mind, however, does not accept the polarity, the interdependence of the opposites like beautiful and ugly, good and evil, etc., and thereby creates a dualism and conflict between the opposites. (DO 20)

ঽঽঽ

So long as the body-mind continues, duality is still there. Whatever the body-mind does in duration, in space-time, is in duality. What is absent in enlightenment is dualism, "me" as a separate entity and "you" as another separate entity. (CS 138)

ঽঽঽ

There can be no manifestation unless it is observed through the body; there can be no observation unless there is the mind; there is no mind unless there is consciousness in the body-mind organism; and where can the consciousness in the body-mind organism come from except from CONSCIOUSNESS, or the SOURCE? There is, therefore, no duality—only UNICITY.

Duality and Space-Time

In fact, there has been neither creation nor destruction. Bondage lasts only as long as mind invests a perceived object with reality. Once that notion disappears, with it goes the supposed bondage. Here, in this objectified creation, only that which is thus objectified grows and decays. It is in this conceptualization and objectification that the duality is conceived as the very basis of the manifestation. Duality is necessary so that manifested objects may be perceived and cognized in a framework of space and time in which the objects are extended. It is essential to bear in mind that while the manifestation thus created is of the nature of mere appearance or illusion, it is real enough in the sense that the manifestation is a reflection in Consciousness. The shadow has no substance or nature of its own, but without the substance the shadow cannot arise. (FT 14)

The Dream and Space-Time

HOLLY *My question is about time. Does time happen all at once, or is it actually a sequence like the body-mind tends to see it?*

RAMESH What happens in a dream, your personal dream? The moment before the dream starts there is no time for Holly. The moment the dream starts there is space and time. Old men dying, rivers and mountains hundreds of thousands of years old—all that happens in the personal dream which a moment before was not there.

Exactly the same thing happens when you wake up— the manifestation is there, the space is there, and the time is there. Space and time are the basis for the manifestation to appear. The mystic has been saying for years and now the physicist is saying it—no object exists unless it is observed. For the three-dimensional object extended in space to be observed, the observation needs time. So unless there is space, the three-dimensional object cannot be extended, and a three-dimensional object extended in space doesn't exist unless it is observed in time. Space-time is the basis for the manifestation and its functioning. Space-time comes along with the manifestation. The dreamed manifestation, a moment before the dream starts, doesn't exist. When the dream starts, things exist.

Divine Hypnosis

INDRANI *There is confusion in my mind, Ramesh. Could you*

please help me? Now, if you say this world is a reflection in Consciousness ...

RAMESH   Yes.

INDRANI   *Yes, but something can only reflect if there is something...*

RAMESH   Yes, Consciousness is all there is.

INDRANI   *Yes, but how does It reflect a world then?*

RAMESH   Consciousness creates the reflection within Itself.

INDRANI   *Oh! An illusory world is that which is being reflected.*

RAMESH   That is correct. When you stand before the mirror, what is seen in the mirror is illusion. It's not there. It can be there only if you are there. So this illusory world as manifestation cannot be there in the absence of Consciousness. The moving pictures cannot be there in the absence of the screen. So, the screen is real. The moving pictures are not real. Consciousness is Reality. Everything is the manifestation, the human beings are part of the manifestation. The functioning of the manifestation is like a dream.

ANNAN   *How do I get in touch with my consciousness and maintain that contact?*

RAMESH   Now, we've just said it is not "your" Consciousness.

ANNAN   *It is not mine.*

RAMESH   It is not "your" Consciousness. Annan wants to

get in touch with "his" Consciousness. What is Annan? To me it is merely the name given to a body-mind organism. So what I see is a body-mind organism which is an object, which is part of the totality of manifestation. You see? And this body-mind organism, this object as part of the manifestation, is an instrument through which the impersonal Consciousness, or Energy, functions. There are various gadgets—fans, lamps, kitchen gadgets—through which electricity functions. So all human beings are merely programmed instruments through which Consciousness, or impersonal Energy, or God, functions.

ANNAN   *How do I get in touch with Consciousness?*

RAMESH   "Who" gets in touch with Consciousness? Consciousness is all there is. If Consciousness is all there is, can there be anything else that can get in touch with Consciousness? Consciousness is the Source of the manifestation, and this body-mind organism which considers itself Annan is part of the manifestation. ...

Now a clever hypnotist can make 2,000 people believe something which is not there is there as a solid entity, can he not? So if a clever hypnotist can make 2,000 people believe there is something solid when there isn't, then is it difficult for the Divine through hypnosis to make each individual body-mind organism think that the world is real, solid? (TM 124-127)

ৰৰৰ

We are constantly being mislead by God— through Divine hypnosis—so that life as we know it may go on. (TM 233)

Destiny

RAMESH ... God's will in respect of each body-mind organism is what I call the destiny of that body-mind organism, stamped at the moment of conception. At the moment of conception the destiny of that conception is stamped.

MARKUS *So you can switch these words, God's will and destiny?*

RAMESH They are the same thing. God's will in respect of each body-mind organism is the destiny. The destiny of a body-mind organism is God's will.

MARKUS *So this says actually "you" can't do anything, just accept.*

RAMESH That is correct, Markus. That is indeed what I am saying. So if a conception is not destined to fructify into a baby, then that conception will be aborted. The mother may decide to abort the conception. If it is born, how long that organism will live is part of the destiny, and during that life span, what will happen is also part of the destiny, which is God's will.

So if a murder happens, what has really happened? What has happened is that one body-mind organism has been killed and another body-mind organism is the instrument through which this killing has happened. The one which was killed—it was the destiny of that body-mind organism to be killed by a particular body-mind organism—that is destiny. Nobody knows how one is going to die. It may be a natural death, it may be an accident, it may be murder, it may be suicide. So which of these four ways will apply to a particular body-mind organism is its destiny, stamped at the moment of conception. If it is the destiny of a body-mind organism to be murdered, that body-mind organism will be murdered. That will be the way that body-mind organism is supposed to die. What happens to the body-mind organism which committed the murder will subsequently also be the destiny of that body-mind organism. Not all crimes are detected. Not all crimes detected are punished. So whether that body-mind organism will be punished or not for the murder which happened through it will be its destiny and the will of God.

There was a body-mind organism called Mother Teresa which was so programmed that only wonderful things happened. Those wonderful things which happened brought a lot of rewards: Nobel Peace Prize, many other awards and any number of acknowledgments. So what has happened? What I am saying is there was no Mother Teresa who received all those awards. Mother Teresa was only the name of the body-mind organism whose destiny it was to receive them.

On the other hand there is a psychopathic organism. The psychopath didn't choose to be a psychopath. But the psychopath has been programmed to do what society and the law calls evil acts, perverted acts. So those acts will happen through that body-mind organism which is programmed to commit such acts. That will be the destiny of that body-mind organism of the psychopath. And the psychopathic organism may or may not be punished, according to its destiny. But my main point is that whether it is the body-mind organism of a Mother Teresa or the body-mind organism of a psychopath, both have been produced by the same Source. We can only accept God's will. We cannot try to understand God's will. Why can we not?

MARKUS   *We cannot try to understand God's will?*

RAMESH   You cannot even begin to try, Markus, for this reason: our intelligence is very limited; our intellect is very limited; whereas God's intellect is all eternity. So how can we, who can only see in a limited way, understand God's will? We cannot.

MARKUS *Nobody can?*

RAMESH Nobody can, because everybody is merely a small part of the total manifestation which is a reflection of the Source. All you can do, as you just said a little while ago, is to accept things as they are. This is it!

MARKUS *As soon as you accept this, there are no questions anymore.*

RAMESH That is the point. Whether you call it acceptance or surrender makes no difference to me. People who are happier to think in terms of God prefer the word "surrender." Those who are more intellectual and prefer to use the word Energy or Source will say "acceptance." It means the same thing. And what is the acceptance and the surrender? What is the *basis* of this acceptance and surrender? That there is truly no "me" who can do anything. What is the final bottom line of acceptance and surrender? That *there is truly no "me" who can do anything.* There is really, truly no "me."

NINA *What about these man-made structures of good and bad, wrong and right, that we spend our whole lives battling—if it is God's will then there is nothing right and there is nothing wrong. The psychopath is doing what is his destiny.*

RAMESH That is correct.

NINA *The right and the wrong is imposed by us on ourselves.*

RAMESH That is correct. That is quite correct. And that imposition of right and wrong for a particular body-mind organism is God's will in respect of that body-mind organism—not an individual but a body-mind organism. You see? It is the destiny of that body-mind organism we call a psychopath for certain things to happen. It was the destiny of a body-mind organism called Mother Teresa for those kinds of actions to happen.

NINA *And the way of a psychopath or a murderer, according to our rules, is to be put into prison or given the death sentence. That is in his destiny?*

RAMESH That is the destiny of that body-mind organism. Quite correct. That is indeed what I am saying. The act that happens is the destiny. The consequences of that act are also destiny.

NINA *So the one that gets away with a heinous crime or the one who gets penalized by his peers for the crime, that is also in his destiny?*

RAMESH And why do you forget the innocent man who gets punished? See, that is also destiny. And how may crimes have there been where innocent people were executed and then later it was realized that they were wrongly executed? That was the destiny of the man to be wrongly accused and executed. (TM 39-42)

ૠૠૠ

BRUCE *Ramesh, I have a question about the concept of destiny. When you refer to destiny, is it the destiny of the body-mind organism?*

RAMESH Yes. Indeed!

SINGH *Does that include or is that similar to the destiny of the ego?*

RAMESH No. The ego has nothing to do with it. It is the destiny of the body-mind organism. The destiny is always of the body-mind organism. The ego, frankly, doesn't exist!

The ego does not have a destiny. (TM 111)

ༀༀༀ

BRENDAN *Then why isn't it the ego that has the destiny? This, the body-mind organism, is just a mechanical ...*

RAMESH   I know. So what happens to the body-mind organism is the destiny of the body-mind organism. Whatever happens in life to that body-mind organism happens only to the body-mind organism—it does not happen to the ego. The ego, because of this hypnosis, thinks, "It is happening to me."

BRENDAN *I thought you said mind and ego are synonymous.*

RAMESH Yes! The thinking mind and the ego are the same. (TM 112-113)

Programming, Conditioning, and Programmed Computer

By programming I mean certain natural characteristics which were stamped at the moment of conception: physical, mental, intuitive, and emotional. And this body-mind organism has been conditioned by the environment. You had no choice about your parents, you had no choice about the genes or DNA, you had no choice about the environment; therefore, you had no choice about the conditioning which this body-mind receives. And by programming, I mean genes and conditioning. (TM 241-242)

ༀༀༀ

MARK *My sense is that there is a relationship between* vasanas *and the ego, if there are a lot of* vasanas *there is a strong ego.*

RAMESH What does *vasana* mean? *Vasana* means inherited tendency.

MARK *Programming?*

RAMESH Inherited tendencies are the programming. In some cases the programming is such that there is great resistance, and in other cases the programming is such that it is wide open—there is great receptivity.

MARK *As a body-mind organism moves through life, you mentioned that the conditioning ...*

RAMESH The conditioning happens all the time. And the new conditioning may alter the old conditioning. New concepts deleting old concepts. As Ramana Maharshi said, that is the only purpose of a concept—to be used as a thorn to remove another thorn imbedded in your foot, and then you throw both thorns away.

ৰৰৰ

RAMESH ... The brain is part of the inert body-mind organism that cannot create anything. It can only receive and react. The brain is a reacting agent, an apparatus.

MARKUS *So this body-mind is receiving and doing?*

RAMESH That's right. So what I'm saying is a thought comes, the brain reacts to that thought, and that reaction is what Markus calls "his" action. Markus sees something or hears something, the brain reacts to it, and that reaction is what Markus calls "his" action. But Markus has no control over what will happen. Markus has no control over what thought will arise. Markus has no control over what he is going to see, or hear, or touch, or smell, or taste. Therefore, Markus has no control over what thought will arise or what he will see. The brain reacts to something over which Markus has no control, and how does the brain react? According to the programming—genes plus conditioning.

If you have a personal computer, you put in an input. What will be the output, Markus? Exactly according to the way it is programmed. What can a personal computer do except bring out an output strictly according to the way it is programmed? And who puts in the input? Not the computer. You put in the input. So with the body-mind organism, which is a programmed instrument or computer, God puts in an input. He makes you hear something, see something. He sends a thought. That is the input.

MARKUS   *What if there is a body-mind organism identifying with its name and who doubts what he or she is going to do? Is it already clear what will happen?*

RAMESH   Be mindful of what happens, Markus. Find out what happens from your personal experience, not because of a concept. From your own personal experience find out whether what you think is "your" action is really someone's action. Or is it merely the reaction of the brain to an input over which you have no control, according to the programming over which you have had no control? (TM 34-35)

ༀༀༀ

ROBERT   *The question I have is about conditioning. What I've been telling people is that in order for them to experience some healing or change, they have to go against their conditioning. I understand, especially now, that intrinsically it's impossible to go against one's conditioning. It just can't happen. Yet in therapy it seems that in some cases people are able to do new things. It seems like change is the ability or the occurrence of something*

38

going on that is not in the conditioning.

RAMESH What you are really saying, Robert, is that in telling them to try and change their conditioning, you are giving them fresh conditioning. What are you getting by sitting here? It's conditioning!—which could change or amend Robert's existing conditioning.

ROBERT *That's very clear.*

RAMESH What is happening now? You are getting fresh conditioning. Make no mistake.

ROBERT *So this is just conditioning?*

RAMESH This additional conditioning changes the attitude.

ROBERT *The conditioning isn't fixed, it's constantly being ...*

RAMESH You're a psychologist?

ROBERT *Yes.*

RAMESH The psychologists tell me that the earliest conditioning is the firmest conditioning and is the basis of the personality. But conditioning is happening all the time, every moment. Whatever you hear, whatever you see is part of the conditioning. And that conditioning can amend the earlier conditioning.

That you must fight the ego is prior conditioning. Now I'm telling you—don't fight the ego. It is useless. The ego will not commit suicide. It is only that Power which created the ego that can destroy the ego. So accept the ego and let it continue as long as it is destined to continue. This is the conditioning that will alter the existing conditioning of being told to fight your ego.

ROBERT *There is no going against conditioning ...*

RAMESH   This is *fresh* conditioning. That's what I'm saying.

ROBERT   *What a great relief that conditioning happens!*

RAMESH   Conditioning is happening all the time. So what you are really trying to do professionally is not to tell them to change their conditioning but to do something. Your telling them to do something may be against their existing conditioning, but you are not really trying to tell them to change their conditioning.

I'm not telling you to change your conditioning. All I'm saying is, according to my concept, accepting the ego means weakening the ego.

ৰৰৰ

RAMESH   Two sages are walking along the road. The programming in one is timidity, and the programming in the other is physical courage. Both see a woman being molested. That is what is seen. That is an event over which neither sage had any control. Upon seeing the woman's desperate situation, the brain in one sage reacts according to the programming and he goes to rescue her. In the process he badly injures her assailant and is arrested and goes to jail. The other sage, because he is programmed to be timid, hesitates and does nothing. The one programmed to be brave accepts the consequences of his actions. Likewise, the timid one accepts the consequences of his action. He doesn't feel guilt or think that he too should have been courageous.

Now the ordinary person would react differently. If brave, he may have done the same thing, but he would also get involved in the consequences of being arrested: I should not have hit the attacker; I should not have even helped the woman. This is involvement. The sage would simply accept the consequences. An ordinary, timid person would feel guilt about not helping or wish he were braver.

This too is involvement. The timid sage would not get involved, he would accept his timidity and the consequences—not wishing he was programmed otherwise or had acted differently.

It is the judging by the ego, the thinking mind, which is the involvement. The working mind just does what it is programmed to do and accepts the consequences.

ཨཨཨ

LARRY *Carrying this example further, let's say a sage is a homosexual and unenlightened.*

RAMESH "Sage is unenlightened," you said?

LARRY *To begin with.*

RAMESH No, then he cannot be a sage. A sage is enlightened.

LARRY *All right, then there is a person who is a homosexual and enlightenment has not happened. There is some evidence that homosexuality is genetic.*

RAMESH Oh, a great deal of evidence I'm told.

LARRY *Time passes and enlightenment happens in that body-mind which is genetically programmed towards homosexuality. So then, that body-mind could be a sage and a homosexual.*

RAMESH Oh yes! Certainly. That would be the programming of that body-mind organism.

LARRY *Okay, so that follows. He wouldn't feel guilt after enlightenment.*

RAMESH That's the point. He wouldn't feel guilt. The destiny would be accepted.

ཨཨཨ

RAMESH What is the difference between anger arising in a sage and anger arising in an ordinary person? Anger arises because the brain *reacts* to what is heard or seen. The brain produces the anger, not the ego. Where does the ego come in? The ego reacts to the reaction of the brain. That is involvement. In the sage the anger arises as a reaction of the brain, but the sage witnesses it taking its course. The anger may result in an action. The sage watches the anger arise and take its action. The sage doesn't say it was "I" who was angry and "I" did this act.

The subsequent reaction to the basic reaction is the ego, the involvement. The original reaction is a physical reaction of the brain. The subsequent reaction is the ego. In the case of the ordinary person, he would say, "'I' was angry. 'I' shouldn't be angry. My doctor has told me not to be angry, so therefore 'I' must do something not to get angry. 'I' must find some way not to get angry. 'I' must control myself." This goes round and round and round. In the case of the sage anger arises and simply takes its course with no involvement.

Here is a specific example in the case of Nisargadatta Maharaj. What happened was someone asked a question. Maharaj's ears heard the question. So hearing of the question happened. The brain reacted to that question and anger arose: "You've been coming here for many years and you ask a stupid question like that?" Anger arose. But what happened? Almost immediately thereafter the same man made a statement that was very humorous, and Maharaj laughed the loudest. So one split second anger arose, and in the next minute laughter arose. In the case of an ordinary man what would have happened? He would have said that he was not going to laugh. But there was no Maharaj to get angry. Anger came and went and laughter took its place.

About fear, it too arises. For example, there are two ordinary people. Fear arises in the case of one, and fear does not arise in the case of the other. Arising of the fear has nothing to do with the ego, but the ego reacts to that fear. And as with anger so with fear, the ordinary person says, "'I' was afraid. 'I' get afraid. 'I' wish 'I' could be like my friend who doesn't become afraid." So the involvement arises because of not being able to accept the programming.

In the case of a sage, fear may also arise. If so, he accepts that the body-mind organism is so programmed that in having a particular kind of experience, fear arises. The fear may make him run away, but in running away the sage will not say, "'I' should not have run away. My friend did not run away. Why did 'I' run away? 'I' should not get afraid." That would be the involvement of the ego—the ego's reaction to the fear.

So there is a basic reaction and also the reaction of the ego. In the case of the sage a basic reaction happens because it is a programmed reaction of the brain. But there is no ego, and therefore there is no involvement of the ego. There is no reaction to the basic reaction by the ego.

Don't forget, this is a concept. It is what I say. You have to find out from your own experience if this concept is acceptable or not. That will depend on God's will and your destiny. It is remarkable how confirmation of what I'm saying is found in the *Bhagavad Gita*. In the *Bhagavad Gita* it says that likes and dislikes arise when the senses come in contact with their respective objects, and that you should not get *involved* in the arising of the likes and dislikes. *That* is the problem. The *involvement* is the problem, not the arising of the likes and dislikes. The arising of the likes and dislikes is a natural thing—getting involved with them is the problem.

The Movie

GERRY *Because the Source manifested the phenomenal world ...*

RAMESH That's right.

GERRY *... through time and space, and because It is outside time and space, not confined by time and space ...*

43

RAMESH   Quite correct.

GERRY ... *the total movie has happened. Therefore my total life has already happened. Thus it is destined. Everything that's going to happen to me must happen because it has already happened.*

RAMESH   That's the whole point of it. Destiny is usually thought of as something that is going to happen in the future. No, no, I've kept on repeating this, as Gerry has again pointed out, and it is stated in the *Bhagavad Gita*: Lord Krishna tells Arjuna, "I have already killed them. You are concerned about having to kill your friends, neighbors, relatives, and even preceptors." But he says that he has already killed them. In other words the movie has already been done: *I* have written the story; *I* have written the script; *I* am playing all the characters in the movie; and *I* am witnessing the movie which is already done.

You see? So whatever we talk about is worthless. And that is exactly what Ramana Maharshi was talking about when he said that there is no creation and no dissolution. It is only a movie. So before the Source created the movie what was there? Nothing! There was no creation. And the movie is not *really* a creation!

Thank you, Gerry. That was good.

ৰৰৰ

DANIELLA   *Why is God doing this? Just for fun?*

RAMESH   Yes! *Lila.* The word in the Hindu philosophy is *lila.* It is God's game. This is a sort of movie He has already made. The movie is there.

DANIELLA   *There's no purpose?*

RAMESH   There is no real purpose. It's entertainment. You see, if a movie is made with all good characters, who is going to see it? You go and see a movie because it creates interest. There's a hero and there's a villain. So in his movie

44

God has created heroes, and villains, and love stories, and tragedies, and comedies. God, or Consciousness, has written the script for the movie, produced the movie, directed the movie, is playing all the characters in the movie—this is the important point—and is suffering and enjoying whatever is happening to each character. Consciousness has made the movie and Consciousness is witnessing the movie. And the characters in the movie are complaining!

ERIC *Hey, I want a better role!*

RAMESH Yes. I want to be a Mother Teresa, I don't want to be a psychopath! That is the whole problem.

HOPE *Shakespeare said all the world's a stage. The players have their entrances and they have their exits.*

RAMESH Yes. That's right. That's all that is happening. If you really see that, that this is a movie which is already there, already finished ...

DANIELLA *For all time?*

RAMESH For all time! There is no way to alter it. That is why I said, "'Who' is complaining?" The character is complaining, but the movie is already done. So my role is already finished.

LAUREL *It is the character's role to complain.*

RAMESH Quite right.

HOPE *Ramesh, don't you think God would let you change roles if you wanted to? I mean, if he wanted to let you change roles.*

RAMESH In this movie a good man can become a bad man; a bad man can become a good man; but it is part of the movie. The movie is already there. An enemy can become a friend; a friend can become an enemy—which is happening in life all the time.

HOPE *But the manifestation does not know.*

RAMESH   The character does not know what is going to happen at the end of the movie.

JAY *This is for all characters.*

RAMESH   For all characters. And the only thing is: a character who has realized that he is only a character does not care anymore.

JAY *And there is no cause and effect, there is no karmic situation which creates the movie for the future?*

RAMESH   Yes. But in the movie, how does the plot develop, Jay? The causation leads from one thing to another thing and that leads to something else—which is the whole plot; which is the design.

JAY *Then there's nothing that can happen haphazardly. It's all cause and effect to keep the movie going on into infinity.*

RAMESH   Yes.

WOLFGANG *Is there any overview of the objective or goal? The sages say that ultimately all sentient beings will be enlightened. Do you subscribe to that?*

RAMESH   No. It is a hopeful concept.

DANIELLA *But isn't it boring for God if all is finished already?*

RAMESH   He will make a new movie. You see the Potential Energy has activated Itself, and when this activation comes to an end—with that burst of energy having exhausted itself—it goes back into the Potential. And then It again activates Itself. (TM 203-205)

4

Ego

RAMESH What is the bondage? The bondage is—"I" am a separate person with free will and responsible for my actions, and therefore "I" must do good things. What is the bondage? The ego is the bondage. "Who" is happy or "who" is unhappy? The ego, the sense of doership. The body can't be happy or unhappy. So the "one" who is happy or unhappy is the ego. And what is liberation? Liberation is the freedom from the alternating sense of happiness and unhappiness. Liberation is the total, final understanding in the heart that there is no doer, no experiencer.

Every religion tells you to get rid of your ego, but the "one" to whom the religions tell to get rid of the ego—*is the ego!* The ego is told to get rid of the ego! But the ego is not going to commit suicide. Therefore the question really is, Who created the ego? That the ego has to be got rid of— agreed. But who created the ego? You didn't create the ego. Where could the ego have come from? Where could it have come from except from the Source! Whether you call that Source Consciousness or Primal Energy or God or Awareness makes no difference, so long as you understand that It is the Source—One without a second.

So the ego has also come from the Source. That is why I call the ego Divine hypnosis. The hypnosis is—"I" consider myself a separate being with a sense of doership. Why has the Source created the hypnosis of separation, because without separation interhuman relationships won't happen. It is only because of this separation that we have friendship

47

and enmity, love and hate. All that arises only because each individual considers himself or herself a separate being. And without interhuman relationships life as we know it would not happen.

Remember, the Source having created this ego, or Divine hypnosis, is in the process of removing the hypnosis in a few cases, not in all cases. So the ego—the sense of separation, the Divine hypnosis, the sense of personal doership—basically has been destroyed by the Source in the case of a few body-mind organisms called sages.

What remains in the case of a body-mind organism called a sage? The programming remains. That's why you may have ten sages, and in each case the sense of personal doership has been demolished, but they differ in life. Why, because the programming is different. In other words, even though the ego is destroyed, the Source continues to use those body-mind organisms of the sages in the same way the Source uses other body-mind organisms—to put in an input and bring out an output. So the body-mind organisms of the sages continue to function exactly like before *but* without the sense of doership and separation.

If the body-mind organism of a sage has the programming to be quick of temper, then that sage before liberation happened got angry very quickly. And after enlightenment the sage continues to become angry very quickly. The programming is for anger to arise. The only difference is that earlier the sage used to say, "I shouldn't get angry with my friends. My friends don't like it. And I'm told I must not get angry because my blood pressure will rise, therefore I'm told that I must control my anger." All that was the *involvement* of the ego, which used to happen before the ego was destroyed. What happens after the ego has been destroyed? When anger arises the sage does not say, "I am angry. I shouldn't get angry." He doesn't say that. The anger that arises and the effect of it is merely witnessed, including the consequences. On the other hand, if something is happening and compassion arises, earlier the ego would have said, "I am a compassionate man and people should respect me." But after the ego is destroyed there is no such thinking. The sage does not think like this. All he sees is compassion arising and taking its course.

The compassion of a sage may take any form. Finding someone hurt he may bandage them, or seeing someone in need he may reach into his pocket and give some money. So the compassion arises and takes its own course, but the sage is never involved in that action as "his" action. That is the only difference according to my concept. The sense of personal doership has been erased forever. He just witnesses things happening not as "my" action or someone else's action. If an action from some other body-mind organism hurts the sage, the hurt will be there. But knowing that no one does anything, Consciousness is all there is, the sage cannot hate anybody. Whom will he hate? All actions are God's actions. Or if you wish to put it another way, all actions are the impersonal functioning of Consciousness. So "whom" will the sage hate? Consciousness? God?

With the ego having been destroyed the sage does not get proud; the sage does not feel guilty; the sage does not hate or envy anybody. So the absence of guilt, pride, hate, envy makes life peaceful. And that is what the search has all been for—peace during the waking state which exists in the deep sleep state. My concept of all spiritual search is to have that peace which prevails during deep sleep even during the waking state, during your ordinary working life. And that kind of peace prevails in your daily life if this happens: there is no ego to feel guilt, pride, hate, or envy.

ૐૐૐ

Every event, every thought, every feeling concerning any "individual" is a movement in Consciousness, *brought about by Consciousness*. (CC 36)

ૐૐૐ

Every thing or object in the manifested universe is a product of Consciousness, both during the illusion when the manifestation appeared to be "real" and after the realization of the Truth... We are nothing but Consciousness, and never have been anything else. Perhaps it would be easier to "understand" the Truth if it is conceived that there never has been any "we" at any time, and that all there is—and has ever been—is Consciousness. "We" think of ourselves, consciously or unconsciously, as sentient beings and therefore as separate from the manifestation: "we" are the subject and the rest of the manifestation is the object. The reality is that "we," as manifested phenomena, are actually nothing but a part of the one manifested universe. What makes us think of ourselves as separate is the fact that the apparent universe becomes *known* to us, as sentient beings, through sentience operating through cognitive faculties. This "sentience," as an aspect of Consciousness in *Itself*, is a direct manifestation of the whole-mind*. And it is for this reason that we cannot get rid of the deepest feeling that "I" am other than the manifested appearance. And so indeed we are, but the illusion (the *maya*) consists in the fact that instead of *collectively* considering ourselves as sentience which enables us to cognize the manifestation (including sentient beings) which has appeared in Consciousness, we consider ourselves as *separate* individual entities. And therein lies our suffering and bondage. As soon as there is realization (awakening to the fact) that we are not separate entities but Consciousness Itself (with sentience acting as the means for cognizing the manifestation), the illusion of separateness—the cause of our suffering and bondage—disappears. There is then the clear apperception that unmanifested, we are Noumenon, and while manifested, we are appearance—no more separate than substance and its form (gold and the gold ornament). Manifestation arises from the Unmanifest and in due course sinks back into the Unmanifest. The human beings *as individuals* are *really* quite

see Glossary

irrelevant, except, of course, as illusory characters in a dream play which is known as "life." (DO 42-43)

Sense of Freedom

ASHIKA *When you speak about how our lives are determined, using the concepts of the robot or the computer, it sounds like it's very limiting—there's no choice, no freedom. But my experience is that I feel filled up with a sense of freedom.*

RAMESH Sure, that's the whole point. So what is that sense of freedom which arises? What kind of freedom is it?

ASHIKA *I am not that computer or the robot.*

RAMESH *Exactly!* That is the whole point. So, freedom from what? Freedom from that which earlier identified itself with the computer. It means freedom from the computer itself, freedom from the identification with the computer. The feeling Ashika has now is that earlier you thought "you" were the computer, and now you know that you are not the computer. That computer is being used by the Source, or God, to bring about such actions as are supposed to happen through that body-mind organism. Isn't that right?

ASHIKA *I used to think that freedom was freedom of choice, to do what I want …*

RAMESH Free will.

ASHIKA *Yes. That all seems to die …*

RAMESH So there is no free will. It does not bring a sense of constriction or freedom.

ASHIKA *There is a totally different freedom—freedom of not being involved at all.*

RAMESH   Yes. Freedom from involvement. Your experience has been that involvement is what causes unhappiness—if there is no involvement there is no unhappiness. So really what you're saying is that the freedom is from unhappiness because the freedom is from involvement. And "who" gets involved? The ego gets involved. *The freedom is the freedom from the ego.* And the ego is the sense of personal doership. So the freedom is *ultimately* the freedom from the sense of personal doership—both for this body-mind organism and other body-mind organisms.

This is remarkable as far as you are concerned. Others may not accept this, but as far as you're concerned the freedom extends to *everybody*. No one has free will. All that happens is that actions happen through the billions of body-mind computers. So there is no need for Ashika to feel guilty or proud or hate anybody. Is that acceptable?

ASHIKA   *Yes.*

RAMESH   This is the freedom that is reflected in your understanding—freedom from guilt, freedom from pride, freedom from hate and envy—which means what? Freedom from involvement. It is the involvement which causes unhappiness—a little bit of happiness, a lot of unhappiness. So accepting what *happens* as something with which Ashika *cannot* be involved *and* over which Ashika has no control at all—this is the freedom that whatever is happening is *beyond* the control of *anyone*. Therefore whatever is happening is just accepted as something which is supposed to happen—and not by the will of any individual.

ASHIKA   *I was feeling confused because there was this tremendous sense of freedom, but it wasn't a sense of freedom from or a freedom to do. It was just this freedom to be.*

RAMESH You see, the freedom from involvement is freedom from the bondage of the ego. The ego is restricted. So the ego who thought earlier that "he" was free to do whatever "he" liked now finds there is no "Ashika" to do what anybody wants. This is the freedom from responsibility, freedom from the sense of personal doership, and freedom from guilt or pride.

This same freedom is translated by the ego as the loss of "its" own personal free will. You see? So really this freedom is itself freedom from the ego, but the ego can't feel this freedom. Ego feels "it" has lost the free will to do whatever it wants to do—which "it" thought "it" had. This was the confusion you felt—the freedom which arose from the loss of the sense of personal doership meant the loss of freedom for the ego. Does that make sense?

ASHIKA *Yes.*

RAMESH I repeat: *Freedom from the sense of personal doership* means loss of freedom for the ego. And that is the confusion, because there is still this identification of the ego with this body-mind organism called Ashika. The ego still remains and feels terribly restricted.

Free Will

RAMESH First you tell me what you mean by "free will."

RON *The notion that "I" can choose between one thing and another.*

RAMESH Yes, but does that include the consequences of what you choose? Your free will is to choose one thing or the other. Does your free will include the actual happening of what you choose?

MARK *No.*

53

RAMESH What use is your apparent free will, Mark? So that free will which is of no use, you have! So what is the free will? To choose. Certainly you can choose, but whether what you choose happens or not is not in your control. That's why when people use these words. I usually stop them and have them tell me what they mean by "free will."

MARK *The logic that you've laid out, which makes sense to me, is that there is a natural unfolding of creation, that once it's set in motion it unfolds in a very complex and determined pattern. And then there's this ego which thinks it can choose one way or the other.*

RAMESH You see, what do you make your choice on? How do you make your choice?

MARK *That would be my question, because I would ask the question, "Who chooses?"*

RAMESH "Who" chooses? The ego chooses. But the ego chooses on what basis? My point is that the ego makes its "choice" *on the programming it has received.*

MARK *And has no control over.*

RAMESH The environmental conditioning over which the ego has no choice.

MARK *Or DNA, or whatever.*

RAMESH That's right, so there is DNA, or the genes, over which you had no choice plus the environmental conditioning over which you have had no choice. It is these two things that I call the programming with which you will make "your" choice. You'll make your choice on what you have been conditioned to think is right or wrong. So if your free will is based on the programming over which you have had no control, then "whose" free will are we talking about?

MARK *So even the free will is a function of the absolute Subject, or the Source?*

RAMESH That's right, or rather the free will that you value so much is based on something over which you have no control.

MARK *That's good. That's really good!*

RAMESH I come back again to the valid question of the ego. The ego has a valid question: In living in society I'm expected to make a choice—do I not make a choice? I say, "Of course you do." But all I'm saying is that the choice you make, consider whether it is really "your" choice or does the choice *happen*?

ཨཨཨ

RAMESH I say, "Thy will be done," which means the human being has no free will. *And yet* I tell you, "Do whatever you like. What more freedom do you want?" Do you have a problem with these apparently contradictory statements? Can you explain why there is no problem for you, Nazneen? If there is no problem, it means they are not truly contradictory statements. Can you explain this? Some people may say they are obviously contradictory.

NAZNEEN *For me it doesn't present a contradiction because whatever has been happening has been happening anyway. "I" haven't been doing anything. So there really is no individual doer, and there never has been an individual doer. So when you say, "Do whatever you like," it means that whatever is going to happen is going to happen.*

RAMESH Wait a minute. To "whom" do I tell, "Do whatever you like"?

NAZNEEN *You're telling the ego.*

RAMESH   I'm still telling the ego which exists. What you just said was that if there is an *understanding* that there is *truly no ego*, then there is no problem. That's correct. But that is not my point.

My question is—Does the ego have a problem when I say, "Do whatever you like. What more freedom do you want?" and yet to the same ego I'm saying, "Thy will be done," meaning you have no free will? Is there a contradiction? The ego asks the question, "How do I live in society if I have no control over my actions?" And my answer to the ego is, "Do whatever you like. What more freedom can you want?"

NAZNEEN   *Yes, but your answer is that whatever you want and whatever you like is what God wants and God likes.*

RAMESH   *That is the point!* But why is it not a problem? That is the issue. And the problem is always, always for the intellect. Any problem is always for the intellect. The intellect says, "You tell me that nothing happens unless it is the will of God. Therefore I have no free will. And yet you tell me to do what I like. What more freedom do I want." So the intellect says that these two concepts are contradictory. How do you explain to the intellect—which is the ego, the thinking mind—that these are not contradictory?

The answer is you may do what you like, but what you like to do is exactly what God wants you to like to do at that moment in the given circumstance. Therefore, there is no contradiction. Do whatever you think you like. And how does God manage that? Through the programming. What you think you like is based on the programming—genes plus conditioning. God acts through the programming.

What use is that total freedom to do what you like to do if what happens is not in your control? To that extent you have no free will.

JAMES   *And therefore the freedom is useless.*

RAMESH Ah! That is the point. That is the conclusion the ego has to come to—the impression of freedom, which it has been under for so many years, is useless.

REINA *But then, nothing really matters.*

RAMESH That is the final conclusion you come to! Nothing really matters. What is the final effect of Self-realization, of enlightenment?—whatever happens, what does it matter. The intellect will say, "How can you tell me nothing matters? Of course it matters." To the intellect everything matters. So "nothing matters" is the conclusion, the answer, the feeling that comes *from the heart*. What the sage feels every moment is—whatever is happening—what does it matter. But the ego says, "Of course it matters."

When the answer finally comes from the heart—nothing that happens really matters—what is the meaning of this? What is the significance of the heart coming to this conclusion? The significance is that whatever the ego perceives as happening—and that it matters—is really an illusion.

So only after the total final understanding is it that *nothing happens*. And if nothing happens what can matter? To "whom"? So you go back to the first line of the saying by Ramana Maharshi as the final truth—"There is no creation, there is no dissolution." If there is no creation, to "whom" can anything matter? You see? So it is not the ego which says, "What does it matter?" Of course it matters to the ego. But when the ego is demolished and the total, final understanding happens, then the real feeling comes up— what does anything that appears, matter? Because whatever appears is just that, only an appearance! What does an appearance matter? What does it matter? What is "it"? The "it" is an appearance. Nothing really happens. Nothing is created. The ultimate understanding is it really doesn't matter.

ༀༀༀ

57

MIRABAI *More and more my experience is that it's not "me" making any decision anyway! Increasingly I have these flashes of the experience that it really is just Consciousness happening—when I say something, I do something, I make a decision. It feels more and more as if decisions are being made—moving my arm, it's predestined. Frequently it feels like that, and this is beginning to give me a sense of that freedom.*

RAMESH Can you explain that a little bit, Mirabai, as you understand it? As you say, the question was asked of Ramana Maharshi: "I raised my arm. Is that also predetermined?" And Ramana Maharshi said, "Yes." *Just one word.* How would you explain that, that even your raising your arm is predestined—predetermined?

EDDIE *It would be a reaction to something at that moment. Even if I say to you or somebody says, "You are raising your arm because you want to," or whatever. I would be reacting to that or I would not react to that. So it is a reaction!*

RAMESH That is *absolutely correct*, Eddie. In other words, why did the man raise his arm? The raising of the arm was the reaction of the brain to what was heard—that everything is predetermined. Just seconds before Ramana Maharshi had said, "Everything is predetermined." That was heard by the man—by that body-mind organism—and the brain reacted: "I have no free will? I can raise my arm." So the raising of the arm was the reaction of the brain to what was heard. It is as much a reaction as scratching when there is an itch.

EDDIE *And even if you say, "I have an itch. I'm not going to scratch. I'm not going to react." That's a reaction.*

RAMESH Correct. Absolutely.

ཨༀཨ

RAMESH But make no mistake. I keep repeating it: All this is a concept. Make no mistake. It is a concept.

WENDELL *But people seek the Truth through that.*

RAMESH Yes.

CINDY *So it's not the truth that there is no free will?*

RAMESH No. I told you: the only Truth is I Am—I Exist. That is the *only* Truth. Everything else is a concept. Rebirth is a concept. Your karma is a concept. "There is no karma which is yours, all that happens is God's will" is a concept. But the concept that only God's will prevails—*that* concept gives rise to a simple life: no guilt, no pride, no hate. The concept "I have free will" leads to frustration and pride and hate.

CRAIG *Ramesh, though it is a concept, I find that most people who believe in free will have not really thought about the whole matter.*

RAMESH That's correct. That is why I say if you believe that you have free will, find out from your own experience in the past six months or six years to what extent your free will has prevailed. From your own experience you'll find that really there's no free will.

WENDELL *Ramesh, if we accept the concept that there's no individual entity, that solves a lot of problems, doesn't it?*

RAMESH It makes life simple, Wendell. How does it make life simple? Because if I am not the *doer* then why should I feel guilty, why should I feel pride, and why should I hate people? So no guilt, no pride, no hate make life simple. I mean other than that, what does one really need in life? Forget about spirituality. Forget about seeking. Forget about enlightenment. What is it that one needs in life? No guilt, no pride, no hate, no envy make life simple. It means *peace*.

You're quite right. If you seek peace in this life, then the only thing to understand is that you are not the doer, that you're truly not responsible for anything that you do. But that doesn't mean that you have to be irresponsible. Because the answer ultimately is do whatever you like according to any standards of morality and responsibility you have. The standards of morality and responsibility are part of the *programming*, and you cannot act other than your programming. (TM 253-254)

Thought, Feeling, and Prayer

RAMESH The thought and the feeling—there is no difference! A thought arises. A feeling arises. No difference. Scientific research shows that what you consider "your" thought arises half a second before you say it is "your" thought, and therefore, you didn't bring about that thought. The thought occurs, and because of that thought the brain mechanically reacts to it as an input into the computer and brings out an output according to the programming. By "programming" I mean you had no choice in being born to particular parents, therefore you had no choice about your genes, DNA. By the same token you had no choice about being born into a particular environment in which you received your conditioning. So this DNA plus environmental conditioning, over which you have had no control, is what I call the programming of this body-mind computer. And what you think is "your" action is merely the Source, or God or Ishwara, putting in an input and the output comes according to the programming. So where is this "Salome" who thinks and prays?

SALOME *No. That is another thing, because when I pray I thank him for these thoughts: "I am extremely grateful that you give me this feeling. It is by your grace that I can think this way and feel this way. Nothing is mine. It is only by your grace that I feel this." So even this prayer is a thank you that I can pray this way.*

RAMESH So that is a prayer made by an individual "me," isn't it? And what I'm saying, Salome, is that there is really no individual "me." Whatever Salome thinks "she" does is merely the mechanical reaction of the brain to an input over which she had no control according to the programming over which she has had no control. But you think "you" are doing this praying.

SALOME *No. As soon as I think this I thank him for giving me the thought because it is not my doing.*

RAMESH So it is still Salome thanking God for giving her the thought and the feeling!

SALOME *So where do you overcome that?*

RAMESH You see, "where do 'you' overcome that?" There is only one way—there is *no action which is Salome's action,* including the praying. Who did the praying? Salome thinks, "I do the praying." And what I'm saying is prayer *happens* as a purely mechanical reaction of the brain to an input. And what is the input? A thought. The brain reacts to that thought and prays. So the prayer *happens.*

ৠৠৠ

JIM *An enlightened being has no control over the thoughts that come?*

RAMESH Are you saying that even the enlightened being— the body-mind organism in which enlightenment has happened—has no control over what thought will come? You are right! That is precisely what I'm saying.

JIM *Is thought not ego?*

RAMESH *Thought* is not the ego! *Thinking* is the ego! (TM 245)

ᘖᘖᘖ

RAMESH "The choosing by Consciousness among the QM [quantum mechanics] possibilities is an unconscious process. A personal awareness of that choice comes about one-half second later than a 'readiness potential' that appears in the brain-wave," says brain surgeon Benjamin Libet. "Thus, there can be no free will, that most precious 'possession' in the West. The Indian sage, Ramana Maharshi, said the same thing."

So as I understand it, quantum mechanics says that nobody can know what is going to happen in the next minute, in the next hour. The flight of a particle you don't know where it is going to end. You cannot predict it. That's what Niels Bohr says according to the theory of uncertainty. When this theory was explained to Albert Einstein, he said that he could find no fault with the theory of uncertainty, which says that you never know what is going to happen at any given time. Albert Einstein said that although he could find no fault with the theory, his conditioning and upbringing would not let him accept the theory of uncertainty. He said, "I find no fault with this theory, but I cannot accept that "God is playing dice with the universe." Then Niels Bohr replied to him, "God is not playing dice with the universe. You think God is playing dice with the universe because you don't have all the information that God has."

You see, God has the full information, he knows what is happening. He sees the whole picture. It's already there. But we don't possess God's knowledge so nothing is certain. From the wave of probability something happens at any moment to anyone. So when the wave collapses something happens. A thought arises, a desire arises, and it takes a split-second for the brain to react to it and for the mind-ego to immediately take possession and say that it is "my" thought, "my" desire. So the desire arises when the quantum wave collapses. The ego accepts it as "its" desire. Now, you tell me if the desire is of the ego or that of Consciousness. (TM 320)

Mind-Intellect

ANNAN *Is the ego also intellectual?*

RAMESH Ego *is* intellectual. Your mind-intellect and the ego are the same. "Me," the ego, and the mind-intellect are the same. They are various names for the same thing which arises in the body-mind organism and creates a feeling of separation, and that feeling of separation causes misery. In deep sleep this feeling of Annan and the mind-intellect does not exist. In deep sleep there is no Annan, there is no Annan's mind; therefore, there is no misery. (TM 126-127)

ৰৰৰ

RAMESH The intellect, the ego, trying to *grasp*, to *grab* the teaching asks, "If I am not the doer, *who* is the doer?!" That is exactly the point. There is only *doing—happening*—no individual doer!

ৰৰৰ

ROHIT *Sir, if manifestation is a reflection of Reality, then the mind is also a reflection of the Reality?*

RAMESH The mind is not separate from Consciousness. The mind is not different. The mind is part of the body-mind organism; the body-mind organism is part of the manifestation; and the manifestation is a reflection of "reality." ...

ROHIT *Actually I feel, sir, one doesn't see the chair. One sees the appearance of a chair, and he gives reality to that appearance.*

RAMESH That's right, the mind gives it ...

ROHIT *Any of your actions are part of the totality of the manifestation.*

RAMESH Correct.

ROHIT *Actually the whole cosmos, the whole existence itself, is supporting all your actions, and therefore you are the world ...*

RAMESH But who is this "you" being talked about?

ROHIT *... There is no "you."*

RAMESH The apparent world exists only so long as someone observes it, and that makes it *apparent*. What makes it *apparent*? Because it is seen. It is observed.

ROHIT *Is then the world only apparent?*

RAMESH The physicists say no object exists unless it is observed.

ROHIT *It may not exist as an object, but otherwise does it remain?*

RAMESH If not as an object, then what else? As an idea in "your" mind?

ROHIT *It will not be distinct. Objects are always distinct.*

RAMESH And that which is now talking is an object in the totality of the manifestation. And the totality of manifestation is observed through a body-mind organism, of which and in which is Consciousness—Consciousness functioning as the mind. So in deep sleep the mind is not there.

ROHIT   *Mind as a subjectivity as in subject-object?*

RAMESH   Mind is the instrument which perceives things. The eyes don't see the world. The mind sees the world through the eyes. The mind hears the world through the ears. The eyes and the ears are merely the mechanical part of it.

ROHIT   *So what remains is only Consciousness?*

RAMESH   What remains is Consciousness, from which lofty angle you started to talk. From that lofty angle you started talking, and now you ask, "Does the manifestation exist if there is no one to observe it?" If all the sentient beings in the world are in deep sleep at the same moment, "who" is to say whether the world exists or not?

ROHIT   *If it does not exist as a manifestation, then how does it exist?*

RAMESH   It doesn't exist!

ROHIT   *Then it is only impersonal Consciousness.*

RAMESH   Yes, all there is is the impersonal Consciousness. (TM 180-183)

Emotions

MAUNA   *Do you mean that for an enlightened person there are no emotions coming up?*

RAMESH   Sure the emotions come. But supposing an emotion

65

came into this body-mind organism. What would I do? Merely notice it. Watch it arising. It is witnessed as if it is somebody else's, *not "mine"*! You see, the emotion which arises is the reaction of the brain and its conditioning and subsequent memories to something which is seen, or smelled, or heard. So someone comes here and keeps asking questions, the brain reacts to that, and a feeling of great compassion arises. It arises, but it is also known that there is nothing I can do to help that person to get rid of those emotions which he is concerned with. The emotion of compassion arises because of the suffering of the other person who is not easily able to accept the teaching. So you see, compassion arises, but along with that compassion is also the understanding that what happens is the destiny of that body-mind organism.

The compassion which arises does not become a burden for me. The fear which arises does not become an anxiety for me because there is no thinking mind thinking it is my responsibility to make him understand. An ordinary teacher would be very much concerned that it is his or her responsibility to make students understand. So there is the thinking mind which is the involvement! (TM 226)

Responsibility

RAMESH   So even if you tentatively accept that any action which you call "my" action is really not "my" action—it is just happening according to God's will—then something which you think "you" have done and therefore caused some harm or grief to someone else is not a reason to feel guilt. In fact, every human being carries an enormous load of guilt. Most of the thoughts that come are, "I wish I hadn't done this, then so-and-so wouldn't have suffered," or "I wouldn't have been frustrated."

MARCUS   *Yes, but there is no guilt ...*

RAMESH So what I'm saying, Markus, is if you truly accept that it was not "your" action anyway, why should you feel guilt? If you truly accept that it was not "your" action and this action has been praised by others, then why should Markus feel proud? If it is not Markus's action at all, and it is *only* something which Markus *sees* as happening, then what I'm saying is there is no guilt, and there is no pride.

MARKUS *There is no guilt. There is even no morality?*

RAMESH Wait a minute, we'll come to that. There is no guilt, there is no pride, and more importantly, if Markus understands that nothing can happen unless it is God's will—it is not Markus's action—then Markus also knows that something which happens through another body-mind organism is not "his" or "her" action. Consequently, whatever action another body-mind organism might think is "his" action affecting you, *you* know that it is *not* "his" action. So how can you call anybody your enemy? How can you hate anybody? How can you envy anybody? Once you accept that no individual does *anything*—actions happen through each body-mind organism according to the way it is programmed by God—then four beautiful things happen: no guilt, no pride, no hate, no envy. Life becomes simple.

Now, that must raise some questions. The main question at this time being: "If I am not responsible for anything, and things just happen, why should I do anything at all? Why should I not remain in bed all day?"

Markus *I was thinking this yesterday.*

RAMESH You see, that is a valid question which the mind-intellect must ask. Who is this "me"? It is the mind-intellect. The mind-intellect is the "Markus." So the mind-intellect, the ego, says, "If I don't do anything, and I am not responsible for anything, why should I do anything at all?

Why should I not lie in bed and do nothing?" The answer to that is very simple, Markus. Markus thought "he" was functioning, but what was really functioning?—the *Energy*, the Universal Energy functioning through this body-mind organism. That is the One which produces actions. So that Universal Energy functioning or operating through this body-mind organism will continue to operate, and that Energy will not let Markus remain idle for any length of time. Some action will happen through this body-mind organism because the Energy will bring it about—physical or mental. So the Universal Energy inside this body-mind organism will continue to bring about actions because that is Its nature. It is the nature of the Universal Energy to produce.

MARKUS *It would also be a bit boring just to be in bed all day.*

RAMESH That is what the mind-intellect says, and this is quite right. That is also another part of it. And what you have said, in fact, is exactly what I have said: it would be boring to lie in bed because of the energy inside—you can't keep that energy suppressed, controlled all the time. You see? So you cannot remain idle. That is one aspect. The second aspect is responsibility. Markus's mind-intellect asks, "If I am not responsible for what I do, why should I not take a machine gun and go out and kill twenty people? If I am not responsible and everything that happens is God's will, why should I not take a machine gun and go out and kill people?"

MARKUS *Yes, but why should I do it?*

RAMESH No, why should you *not*? Why should you not do it since you are not responsible? The point is if you are not responsible for "your" actions, why should you *not* do this? I'm taking an extreme case. You see, the answer to that, again, is that the basic misconception is you are saying why should "you" not do this and kill people? But what actually happens is that there is *no* "you" to do anything.

MARKUS *If there is someone who is shooting twenty people, is this also God's will?*

RAMESH It *is*, Markus. That is what I am saying. And therefore, what I am also saying is "you" cannot do it because this body-mind organism is not programmed to kill twenty innocent people. So how can this body-mind do such a thing simply because the brain hears that "you" are not responsible?

MARKUS *So there is no question actually of you just sitting in bed and doing nothing, because anyway you can't do anything against God's will.*

RAMESH That's right. So what remains is the question of responsibility. A murderer can say, "Yes, the murder happened, but this teaching tells me that 'I' have not committed the murder, God has committed the murder. Why should I be punished?" That is the next question. You see? The answer to that is very simple—God's will in respect of each body-mind organism is what I call the destiny of that body-mind organism, stamped at the moment of conception. (TM 36-39)

ৰৰৰ

RAMESH Mitra, I noticed yesterday that there was considerable receptivity. There was no resistance. There was much acceptance of what was said.

MITRA *My identity has always been based on what I know. I know this and I know that. Yesterday it went straight here that I know nothing.*

RAMESH How do you mean that you know nothing?

MITRA *I do healing. Last night a cousin was not feeling well and she asked me to give a session. I put my hands out, and there was no longer this worry about trying to control the result. Usually there is this thing that "Oh, I hope she'll do well. I hope she'll be fine," but that doesn't seem to happen any more.*

RAMESH Underlying that feeling "I hope she will be well," what is the real feeling?

MITRA *I am the doer.*

RAMESH I hope "I" shall be able to cure her. Isn't it?

MITRA *That wasn't there last night. It just wasn't there.*

RAMESH So you had the feeling that whatever was happening was happening, and whether she got cured or not ...

MITRA *That was her destiny.*

RAMESH That's right. It didn't depend on "you." It depended on her destiny.

MITRA *It was so freeing.*

RAMESH "It was so freeing." Yes! What was the freedom from? That freedom was from responsibility, that it was your responsibility to cure her.

MITRA *And that can be so heavy.*

RAMESH Ohhhh! Heavy!!

MITRA *Terrible.*

RAMESH So this freedom we're talking about is freedom from responsibility, freedom from guilt, and freedom from pride. But freedom from responsibility does *not mean* freedom from consequences. You understand what I'm saying?

MITRA *Yes. But they are not connected, are they?*

RAMESH They are not connected. You see there is freedom from responsibility—"responsibility" refers to the person. Consequences are just *happening, over which you have no control.*

MITRA *You said yesterday that events happen and deeds are done.*

RAMESH Yes, and therefore I keep repeating that a deed has consequences, but the consequences cannot be predicted. A crime is committed; it is detected; the crime is punished. A crime happens; it is not detected; it is not punished. A crime is not done, and yet the person is punished. So what the consequences will be, no one really knows.

Death - God's Will Prevails

RAMESH God's will does prevail in *everything*, from the smallest thing to the biggest event. That is my concept. Yesterday, the Australian missionary and his two children were burned to death in a car. Did you read the widow's remarks? They moved me greatly. She said, "Each human being has a life span given by God, no one can change it." And she said this not when it happened to someone else but when it happened to her own husband and two children. I was astonished at the depth of the understanding from the heart. What she was saying is that the life span of each body-mind organism is God-given, and no one can change it.

So what I'm saying is God's will prevails in the smallest thing and the biggest event. God's will prevailed when the manifestation happened, and it's God's will when the manifestation will disappear into nothingness again.

KAREN *My question is what happens at death. What is death?*

RAMESH What happens is that which existed before the birth continues to exist after the death of a body-mind object. An object is created. An object is destroyed.

KAREN *Is there awareness before birth and after death?*

RAMESH So that Awareness is the Source. The Source has always been there.

KAREN *I think what you are saying is that for you it wouldn't make any difference whether you are alive or dead.*

RAMESH Yes. Exactly. No difference at all. Who is alive or dead makes no difference. An object is created and an object will be destroyed. The Source creates an object, and the Source destroys the object. The span of life of an object is determined by the Source.

KAREN *This is tricky because for you it doesn't matter.*

RAMESH Consciousness is all there is. And there is no "you"—another—to be that Consciousness. All there is is Consciousness. The real problem is "who" wants to know? All there is is the Source. So "who" is this who wants to know anything? If the Source is all there is, "who" is this who wants to know anything? It is only the ego, and the ego is a fiction, Divine hypnosis. The ego is created by the Source through Divine hypnosis so that between the egos interhuman relationships should happen and life as we know it, which is described as an illusion, should happen.

All there is is the Source. Everything else is an appearance, an illusion. And this "Karen" that wants to know is part of the illusion.

KAREN   *The Source has no desire to know ...*

RAMESH   What can Source know? For something to be known there has to be a subject and an object, and the Source is all there is. So where is the object for the Source, or whatever name you give it, to know?

ཨཨཨ

TIM   *I have something I want to share with you, it's my fear of death. About one year ago I found I had cancer, and then I had surgery. When this happened the fear of death was very strong. Now when I get some pains in my body I think, "Oh my God, I'm dying again," and the fear comes. I wanted to know what you could say to me.*

RAMESH   The only thing I can tell you is what Ramana Maharshi said. Someone stated to him, "I'm afraid of death." So he replied, "Were you ever born? You are afraid of dying, were you ever born?" Only that which is born will die, and that which is born has been dying for thousands of years. Objects have been born and dying for thousands of years. You see? So, "Were you ever born?" was what Ramana Maharshi answered. What was born was a body-mind object, and body-mind objects have been dying for thousands of years. So something which has been going on for thousands of years, why be concerned about it?

The whole point is that you are not that object. You identify yourself with that object and say, "I am this," and therefore you are afraid. In any case this body is going to die sometime, isn't it? It's not going to live forever. This body is going to die just as all these bodies sitting here are going to die, as all bodies have been dying for thousands of years. I repeat, it's something that has been going on for thousands of years, and will continue to be. Why bother about it? Why say, "*I'm* going to die"? A body is going to die, of course it's going to die. Sometime it's got to die. So accepting that the body that was born is bound to die and that there is no "you" to die ...

TIM *That part I don't know.*

RAMESH Of course you don't know. You can just wait and see what happens. You have heard this. Perhaps listening to this *may* produce some effect. I hope so.

ৰৰৰ

RAMESH If you like deep sleep, why are you afraid of death? In deep sleep isn't Vimar dead?

VIMAR *I have no memory of deep sleep so I can't..*

RAMESH So when you are dead you won't have any memory of being dead!

VIMAR *It seems when I look at this fear, when the existence of identity is threatened, it brings tremendous turmoil.*

RAMESH Sure! The ego doesn't want to be killed! But I tell you why you are not afraid of deep sleep, because *you think you know* that you are going to wake up. But you don't really know. Deep sleep by itself is enjoyable and is wanted so much because in deep sleep the ego is not there. It is not that the ego enjoys deep sleep. No, the ego does not enjoy deep sleep, because in deep sleep the *ego doesn't exist*. There is peace in deep sleep. There is no ego enjoying any peace in deep sleep. In fact, the peace you have in deep sleep really means the absence of the ego. The ego is absent in deep sleep, so why be afraid of the absence of the ego permanently?

All I'm saying is, there is no need to be afraid of death. Death is like deep sleep and means peace! That's what death really is—it means peace. But the ego doesn't know that, and that is why the ego is afraid. The ego thinks it is enjoying the peace in deep sleep, but the peace in deep sleep exists because there is absence of the ego. And death is simply a longer deep sleep. Oh, yes.

That is why I keep repeating: anything that any sage has said at any time, anything any scripture or any religion has said at any time is a concept. A concept being something some people will accept, some people will not.

ৰৰৰ

RAMESH What you did not understand is that the ego can be annihilated and yet Catherine can live on. Is that what you are saying?

CATHERINE *Yes.*

RAMESH It was your understanding before coming here that if the ego was annihilated, then Catherine could no longer exist, that this body-mind organism could no longer function. It was your understanding that only when the body-mind died could the ego be annihilated.

CATHERINE *Yes. And of course this caused a lot of fear. I believed that one day I had to let go of my ego, and at the same time I would be dead.*

RAMESH You must have heard me say several times that after Self-realization happened in the body-mind organism called Ramana Maharshi it continued living for fifty years. And for the body-mind organism to continue living, identification with the name and form had to be there. Therefore, if someone called Ramana Maharshi "Swami" or "Bhagwan," he would respond. That he responded to his name being called obviously meant that there had to be identification not only with the body but with the name.

CATHERINE   *That makes it much simpler, and it's not so frightening any more.*

RAMESH   What was the fear about?

CATHERINE   *Of dying.*

RAMESH   Enlightenment may happen if it is God's will and the destiny of this body-mind organism, but Catherine would still continue to live as this body-mind organism. If somebody would call Catherine by name, Catherine would respond. So Catherine would still have to live her life in society very much alive. That's the understanding now, isn't it?

CATHERINE   *That's true. And probably with the same guilt feelings as before.*

RAMESH   That is not so. That's why you've not understood properly. If enlightenment happens, Catherine will live her life without the feeling of guilt—which there used to be before, because Catherine thought that she was the doer. So with the understanding that Catherine is not the doer, Catherine lives in this world without the sense of guilt, pride, hate, or envy. For enlightenment to happen, Catherine doesn't have to die.

Births - Reincarnation

SCOTT   *In one aspect you say that there is nothing, it all comes from nothing, it goes back to nothing. And at another point in a book you say something about reincarnation, which I know is conceptual. But I didn't understand why you said this. It was contradictory to me because I know no individual ego or encapsulated ego continues—there is no continuation. It's all back to nothing.*

RAMESH   Again to use Buddha's words: "There is no soul." Therefore there is no soul to go into another [birth].

SCOTT   *I guess that is why people want to cling to life and want the idea of another life. This way there is some certainty for something uncertain.*

RAMESH   The intellect likes to think of rebirth because the ego does not want to die. The ego says, "I know this body is going to die, but I don't want to die."

SCOTT   *I appreciate your straight forwardness. It's really nice.*

RAMESH   My point is, what is rebirth based on? The theory of rebirth is based on the "doing" by an individual. If the actions of an individual in a particular life are so good, he will have a very good next birth. If you are suffering in this birth that is because in your previous birth you did a lot of bad things. According to the theory of rebirth, the ego does not die, because the ego is the one who is "doing" things.

SCOTT   *That's an illusion.*

RAMESH   Yes. But only *if* you accept the illusion! The intellects of many people don't accept it. In these cases the intellects are appeased—ah, at least there is some basis for my suffering. There is some basis for a child being born handicapped, for someone being born a millionaire. The intellect says, "Now I know why there is a millionaire and I'm a pauper." The intellect accepts it. But my question is this—"Who" enjoys the fruits of the good or bad actions? It's a different ego in a different body.

ཨྱཨྱཨྱ

The future body's personality will be drawn from the totality of the universal Consciousness which is the collection of all the "clouds of images" that keep on getting generated. This total collection gets distributed among new bodies as they are being created, with certain given characteristics which will produce precisely those actions which are necessary to the script of the Divine playwright. No individual is concerned as an individual with any previous entity.

In regard to "I" and "me," there is perhaps a certain misunderstanding. When the "I" is spoken of as the real thing and the "me" as an imposter, a wrong impression is likely to be created that each "me" has a real "I." That is not so. There are billions of "me"s but only one "I"—and even that is a concept! What a Joke!! (CW 99-100)

5

Working Mind and Thinking Mind

RAMESH   Ramana Maharshi said, "Mind is a collection of thoughts." He must have been speaking in Tamil. In my case the concepts of a working mind and thinking mind arose which people have found very useful for understanding. When Ramana Maharshi referred to the mind he was referring to the thinking mind. The thinking mind is a series of personal thoughts and what I call horizontal thinking. Ramana Maharshi said "collection of thoughts," which is involvement in both cases. Horizontal thinking is involvement.

BRENDAN   *But Ramesh, Nisargadatta Maharaj said, "Mind is the content of the Consciousness."*

RAMESH   Yes. That is to say Consciousness is the source of the mind. Where does the mind arise? Where does thinking arise? Only if you are conscious.

BRENDAN   *How can you differentiate between ego and mind?*

RAMESH   You can't. They are the same. The thinking mind and the ego are the same. They are synonyms. ...

SINGH   *So when you say body-mind organism, you include mind.*

RAMESH   In the body-mind organism mind can be both working mind and thinking mind. In the ordinary case it is both the working mind and the thinking mind. In the case of a sage it is only the working mind.

SINGH   *Is the body-mind organism like the program in a data machine which produces thinking?*

RAMESH   The thinking happens according to the way that the body-mind organism has been programmed. The thought will arise as God's input into a particular body-mind organism. Why does a thought occur? Because that is supposed to produce an output. So the equation $E=MC^2$ was there all the time, but it was only that body-mind organism named Einstein which was programmed to receive the equation, that got that thought.

BRENDAN   *When you use the term "body-mind organism," you don't mean mind?*

RAMESH   The term "body-mind organism" means body and, in the case of an ordinary person, both the working mind and the thinking mind, but only the working mind in the case of a sage. (TM 112-113)

ৰৰৰ

RAMESH   The wanting to know is the individual sense of doership—"'I' want to know." Therefore Ramana Maharshi repeatedly said, "If the question arises, do not try to answer the question. Find out who wants to know." If you really go into "who wants to know," the "who" will disappear because there is truly no "who."

The arising of the question is not in your control, or whether you take delivery of that question and get yourself horizontally involved. The arising of the question is a vertical happening. Getting *involved* in that question is a horizontal involvement. So the horizontal involvement is avoided with this question: "'Who' wants to know?"

GAIL *So going into who you are, is that a horizontal activity?*

RAMESH   You see, the asking the question "Who wants to know?" is the working mind. The arising of the question is vertical, the involvement of the *thinking mind is horizontal.* The working mind is *not* horizontal. The working mind is in the Present Moment. So in the Present Moment the working mind asks the question "Who wants to know?" and if the thinking mind doesn't come in and try to answer the question, then the "who" disappears. That is the theory of it. (TM 216)

ཨྃཨྃཨྃ

RAMESH   What was the message which you think you got from *I Am That?*

FREDDIE *Not to hold on to anything, but I can see that my mind acts like a monkey. It always needs to grasp, and if it lets go it grasps again. It's always busy.*

RAMESH   But did *I Am That* tell you to quieten the mind? Which as you say is like a monkey. I think what the book told you was that the problem is the monkey mind. It didn't tell you *how* to quieten it. You've come here 5,000 miles, is there something you expect from me?

FREDDIE *There are expectations that maybe you will turn my mind off.*

RAMESH   Press the button on the remote control and the monkey mind just stops. But tell me, Freddie, if I were able to do that, how will Freddie live his life without the mind?

FREDDIE *I have the idea that life will become easier.*

RAMESH   Quite correct. Life will indeed become simpler without the monkey mind. So what you want turned off is not the mind as such but the monkey mind. For this reason I have a concept which says there are two aspects to the mind. One is the monkey mind—the thinking mind— the mind which asks questions, provides answers, and asks further questions of those answers and goes on and on and on. That is the monkey mind, or what I call the *thinking mind.*

There is another aspect of the mind I call the *working mind.* It is the working mind that is necessary for Freddie to live his life. The working mind is *only focused* with doing what needs to be done *at the moment in the circumstances.* It is *not concerned,* not even with whether the work that is being done is necessary or not. Nor is it concerned with the consequences. It is only focused on doing the job that is being done, and it is not concerned with "who" is doing the job.

It is the thinking mind which says, "'I' am doing this work, and 'I' must find out what the consequences are going to be." So the thinking mind always thinks about the consequences in the future. The working mind is not concerned with the future.

Why is the working mind not concerned with the future? Because the "one" who is concerned with the consequences of the future is the thinking mind, the ego. In the working mind there is *no individual,* no ego, who does the work. So in the working mind if there is no individual *doing* the work, then "who" is to worry about the consequences? In the working mind there is no individual worker—the work is just *being done.*

The individual "doer" is the thinking mind wanting to know: After the work is done, what is going to happen to me? The "me" is the thinking mind, the ego. The ego, according to my concept, is the identification with the name and form as an individual with the sense of doership— whatever happens to this body "I" am doing it, and "I" am the one who is going to suffer the consequences.

FREDDIE   *There is always this longing to make the best decision and to get the best out of it—always, always, always.*

RAMESH   So it is always the "me"—the ego, the "doer"—who says, "'I' am doing the work." According to my concept, the only way the thinking mind—the monkey mind, the conceptualizing mind—can be stilled is if there is *total unconditional acceptance* that there is *no individual doer*. Everything just happens. As long as there is an individual doer who thinks "he" is doing it, then "he" is bound to think and be concerned about responsibility and consequences. This is the thinking mind. But attention can be given to the work at hand without "you" feeling "you" are the doer. That is the working mind.

The real problem is how does Freddie arrive at the *total, unconditional acceptance* that Freddie *never is* the doer, that the doing is *just happening*? Through practical and personal experience. All the doing that Freddie thinks is "his" doing is not because of Freddie but in spite of Freddie! And you know that because Freddie has not been getting what he wanted all the time. So what *happens* is never in Freddie's control, and that you know from practical experience, personal experience. When will Freddie not feel the burden of responsibility and consequences? Only when Freddie is totally convinced that he was not the doer of any action that happened. Freddie is never the doer, and not only Freddie but *no one* is ever the doer. No human being is a doer.

FREDDIE   *Who has come to this conclusion?*

RAMESH   Quite right. The "one" who has come to this conclusion in the beginning is the *ego*, the "one" who thought "he" was the doer. Gradually what will happen is the "I," the ego, which came to the conclusion that "he" doesn't exist will then, over a period of time, find more and more from personal experience that "he" does nothing.

83

Then the ego becomes weaker and weaker, and if it is the will of the Source, the ego collapses.

If the ego collapses, how does this body-mind organism function? The answer is—the body-mind organism will continue to function exactly as it was functioning before. Before it was the Source that was functioning through this body-mind organism, and in the future the Source will continue to function through this body-mind organism. Earlier Freddie thought "he" was functioning. Now Freddie knows "he" is not functioning. The functioning itself, as such, will continue in the future exactly as in the past.

FREDDIE *There is this belief that I have to take care of myself.*

RAMESH That's right. So that which takes care of itself is the working mind. The working mind continues to do what is necessary in the circumstances. Therefore, Freddie still continues as someone accepted by society as responsible for his actions. So what happens? A deed happens, an action happens, and the deed or action is the will of God, or the Source. The will of God in respect of each body-mind object is what I call the destiny of that body-mind object stamped at the moment of conception.

So what is life? According to my concept life is just a multitude of body-mind objects through which the Source is functioning. We can only accept what is happening. We can never know *why* the Source is doing what It is doing. Why? Because if you want to know why God is doing what he is doing, then what is really happening is the created object wanting to know the will of the creator Subject. How is it possible? So the created object which has been endowed with the dubious gift of the ego—the sense of doership, the thinking mind—can only accept the magnificence of God's creation. The object and the ego *cannot even try* to understand why God has done what God has done, because the created object *can never know* the will of the creator Subject.

ॐॐॐ

84

SHEN *Do you say that we should get rid of the thinking mind?*

RAMESH No, I don't. "Who" is to get rid of the thinking mind? The "one" who is supposed to get rid of the thinking mind is the ego. So if it is the will of God and the destiny of that body-mind organism the thinking mind *will—be—got—rid—of!* "You" cannot get rid of the thinking mind. "You" are the thinking mind. And the thinking mind goes when and if you are able to analyze your actions and come to the conclusion that "you" are really not doing anything.

SHEN *But sometimes its necessary to see ahead.*

RAMESH Yes. You mean you have to plan things. Of course. Suppose the sage has to catch a plane at midnight. He will plan when it is best to leave for the airport, when to have dinner prior to leaving, when to arrange for the car. All this is the planning of the working mind. It's not the thinking mind. But the thinking mind is there in the case of the ordinary person doing the same planning. Where is the difference? The ordinary person says, "I've done this planning; suppose the taxi has a flat tire; suppose I'm not able to reach there; suppose the plane doesn't leave; suppose the plane crashes." All that is the thinking mind, which doesn't happen in the case of a sage. He does what is supposed to be done and knows that whatever happens in the future is not in his control.

SHEN *This sounds very reasonable and logical, but it really doesn't come inside.*

RAMESH So it goes inside only when you do the sadhana or practice of analyzing your actions and finding out whether it is "Shen" who is doing the actions or whether the actions are just *happening*. And if the actions are happening and you come to the conclusion day after day that actions just *happen*, that "Shen" has not been doing anything, then the question arises—if "Shen" is not doing anything "who" is "Shen"? Who am I? The question arises and the answer arises from the same Source—there is no "Shen." The point is that actions are happening through the body-mind organism not according to "Shen's" will but according to the will of the Source. So Shen merely watches whatever is happening not as "Shen's" actions.

PREM *I don't really have any questions. I have curiosity, I suppose, but no burning questions.*

RAMESH   Curiosity is the thinking mind. Thinking mind asks a question. Thinking mind provides an answer. Then the thinking mind provides further questions based on the answer, and the thinking mind provides further answers, and then further questions. You see?

ᘒᘒᘒ

RAMESH   The sage considers the consequences in making a judgment—*in making a plan!* The flight may be missed regardless of the working mind's planning. The sage is not concerned with the consequences of missing the flight. That is why the Sufi says, "Trust in God, but tie up your camel!" It is the working mind that ties up the camel and makes sure that the rope is properly tied. After that it is the thinking mind that is concerned with what happens if somebody steals the camel. (TM 229-230)

6

Seeking

RAMESH My concept is this. Ever since a baby is born and seeks its mother's breast intuitively, life is nothing but seeking—but there has *never been* a seeker. What kind of seeking happens depends on the programming, over which you have no control. There are some people who consider themselves seekers of money. Some seek fame. Some seek power. And some seek, among other things, God. This kind of seeking, let's call it spiritual seeking, or seeking God, or seeking freedom from the ego—what you call it is immaterial—is happening to these body-mind organisms sitting here because they are programmed for this kind of seeking to happen.

The seeking begins with an individual ego—seeker—seeking enlightenment, or Self-realization, as an object which will give him or her more pleasure than he or she can ever imagine getting from the material world. That is where it starts. The seeking by the ego for enlightenment can end *not* with intellectual understanding but *only* with the *absolute understanding intuited in the heart* that there never was a seeker, a doer—there never was a seeker for any seeking. There is seeking but no individual seeker. There is doing but no individual doer thereof. That is the end of it! And the end of the seeking can be brought about only by that Power which started the seeking.

DINESH   *Can we interpret "there never was a seeker" as a deception?*

RAMESH   Why use the word "deception"? If you use the word "deception," then I would say life and living are a deception which is what Ramana Maharshi has put in more respectable words: "There is no creation. There is no dissolution."

There never has been a creation, meaning "the creation" is an illusion. The whole creation is an illusion. That is the final understanding you get to. Until then, life is very real. And if life is real then the human being is very real with responsibilities. But make no mistake, the human being is merely a programmed computer—billions of uniquely programmed computers through which the Source is functioning.

ཨཨཨ

RAMESH   Seeking *happens.* "You" didn't start the seeking. Ramana Maharshi said it this way, "Your head is already in the tiger's mouth." You didn't put it there. The seeking has begun because it was God's will, or the will of the Source, that seeking should happen through a body-mind organism. And how that seeking progresses is obviously not in "your" hands. It's in the hands of the Power that started the seeking. So leave God's business to God.

ཨཨཨ

You are quite correct in saying that "at the early stages at least, the paradox is that for the ego to disappear it must first come to understand itself." The mind-intellect must necessarily be used in the early stages to try to understand the What-Is. Then the intellect comes to realize its own limitations, and with this, surrender—intellect eventually becomes merged in intuition. (CC 25)

ཨཨཨ

RAMESH Why does God select a particular body-mind organism for the receptivity to happen? There is no answer to why. The only response is that the created object cannot possibly know the will of the creator Subjectivity. But I've always felt the question of *how*, concerning spiritual seeking, is justified. The teacher to the extent it is possible should help with how—*why* is out of the question.

ཨཨཨ

RAMESH So Lord Krishna says: "Out of thousands there is hardly one who seeks Me, and among those who are seeking, hardly one knows Me in principle." Now, who decides, Markus, who will do the seeking? In fact, the seeking itself is God's will, God's grace.

You think "you" are a seeker. Markus thinks "he" is a seeker seeking God, but the seeking was not Markus's choice. Markus is, you can say, lucky or fortunate that the Source, or God, decided that the seeking would begin in this body-mind organism. So the seeking began not because Markus decided at some point, "From tomorrow I will seek the truth." In fact, the seeking has happened *in spite of Markus*. The seeking is really misery, isn't it? By and large?

MARKUS *The seeking itself—it is, yes.*

RAMESH The seeking itself is misery. Why should Markus choose to be miserable? So what I am saying is the seeking has begun. The seeking begins with a Markus thinking, "I am seeking God, or enlightenment, or peace," or whatever you call it. The seeking begins with Markus thinking "he" is doing the seeking, and the seeking can end *only* when there is the realization that there never was a seeker. The seeking is God's grace and the realization is God's grace, or the will of the Source.

So the seeking begins with an individual thinking "he" is the seeker and cannot end until there is the firm realization that there never was a seeker. Truly, there is no Markus other than a name given to a body-mind organism. In other words, the seeking ends only when there is the realization— there never was a thinker, thinking was happening; there never was a doer, doing was happening; there never was an experiencer, experiencing was happening. Thinking, doing, experiencing are all part of the functioning of manifestation which can only happen through a body-mind organism.

Why did the seeking for God happen in this body-mind organism, whereas in some other body-mind organism the seeking is for money? He only seeks money, and he thinks that Markus is crazy looking for something in the air, that Markus would be much happier if he sought money or power or fame. Now, why is seeking money happening through one body-mind organism, and why is seeking God or Truth happening through this body-mind organism called Markus?

MARKUS   *This is God's will.*

RAMESH   This is what I call God's will or the intention of the Source. (TM 32-33)

What Is Enlightenment? Peace of Deep Sleep

RAMESH   So what is the search for? The spiritual search is for that peace which exists in deep sleep and having it even in the waking state. What is the basis of that peace in deep sleep? It is the non-existence of Elaine as the doer. So how can that peace happen in the waking state? Only when Elaine disappears as a doer, as an individual doer who believes "'I' am in control of 'my' life. 'I' do things. Everything that happens through this body-mind organism are 'my' actions."

ELAINE   *In deep sleep there's no personal awareness.*

RAMESH   The personal awareness is the sense of doership. You see? So the question really is: "How can Elaine enjoy that peace which exists in deep sleep in the waking state?" And the answer is only when there is the total acceptance that what functions is the body-mind organism, and there is no Elaine doing anything. When this happens the sense of personal doership is annihilated.

When the understanding is that whatever happens through any body-mind organism is merely witnessed as the impersonal functioning of Consciousness, or the impersonal functioning of Totality; then the sense of a personal Elaine is not there, and the same peace exists in the waking state which exists in deep sleep. But this happens only when there is total, unconditional acceptance that there is no individual doer. And the happening of that acceptance is not in your control. (TM 343)

ᴅᴅᴅ

TIM   *Acceptance has nothing to do with your spiritual insight?*

RAMESH   "Whose" spiritual insight? That is the problem. "Whose" spiritual insight is the problem.

Subject - Pseudo-Subject

RAMESH   What is seeking? Seeking is "you" wanting to know God. Whatever you know is an object, and you are the subject. So if you want to know God, what does it mean? You are the subject and God is the object, but what exists is the other way around. God is the Subject and you are the object. So how can an object know the Subject? In trying to know God, what the object has done is usurp the subjectivity of God, and what is worse—this pseudo-subject having usurped the subjectivity of God has turned God into an object that the pseudo-subject wants to know. Therefore, the more the seeker tries to seek God, the more frustrated he becomes.

After the talk there are some bhajans being sung, and one of the bhajans is by a sage who put it so easily and beautifully. He said, "I went to know God and returned *being* God." In other words, the object tried to know God, but what really happened was the object disappeared into pure Subjectivity. It is the thinking mind that wants to know God, and the thinking mind, the ego, disappears when there is the realization that there has never been a doer, a seeker.

The *total, unconditional, final acceptance* happens *only* when there is no individual acceptor who says, "'I' accept that 'I' am not the doer." This personal acceptance is not what I'm talking about. The acceptance I'm speaking of is the *impersonal* acceptance in which there is no individual acceptor, or knower. And if the one who wanted to know God has disappeared, then what has happened? It was destiny and God's will that happened—the one who wanted to know God has become God, because God is all there is—the seeker and the seeking have been wiped out. This is my concept.

ॐॐॐ

The one observer is, of course, Consciousness—universal Consciousness—in which has appeared, like a network of waves on the ocean, the totality of the phenomenal manifestation. Universal Consciousness (subjective Noumenon) is, therefore, the only observer (as pure Subjectivity) and everything else in the manifestation is an object. But in life, because of identification with the body, each human being forgets that he is as much of an object as the other objects which he observes. He assumes the subjectivity of the absolute Noumenon and considers himself the observer of the other observed object. By so usurping the subjectivity of the one absolute Subject, the human being commits the original sin and therefore comes under bondage. In other words, universal Consciousness having conditioned Itself as the personal or individual consciousness by identification with a separate entity, considers the person, the limited ego, as the subject observer. As soon as this mistaken identity is realized and the true identity as the one Subject—or witness—is established, the bondage disappears, there is enlightenment. In brief, the "me" (in opposition to the "other") disappears, and in its place shines the "I" as the one formless eternal observer Subject. (DO 22-23)

Ego Is Not God – Never Has Been a Seeker

MIRABAI *And then the ego is God too, right? Is not the ego God as well?*

RAMESH The ego *is not* God because the ego does not exist! But if you mean where could the ego have come from except from the Source or God, then yes, God created the ego. God created the ego through what I call Divine hypnosis. God creates the ego and God is destroying the ego, not in each case but in some cases where the seeking is happening. That is why I say to the seeker, "The most important thing that the seeker has to understand is that 'he' or 'she' has never been a seeker." So I always say that the seeking begins with a seeker seeking enlightenment as something that will give him or her more happiness than anything in the world has given. That's how it begins.

EDDIE *Is it the ego itself that thinks it exists, that thinks it is seeking?*

RAMESH Of course! Of course! Therefore the ego says, "'I' am doing things, 'I' am in control of my life."

ৡৡৡ

93

PREM *You say that in one moment there is the ordinary man and in the next moment there is a realized man?*

RAMESH "He" is *not* a realized man, Prem. Understand that "he" is *not* a Self-realized man. And this is *most* important to understand.

Why Ego Asks Questions

RAMESH The whole point is that any question is asked by the ego. Why does the ego ask the question? Because the ego wants to achieve enlightenment. Why does the ego ask the question? Because the ego is the seeker. So seeking is happening through a particular ego, and the ego—through whom the seeking is happening—didn't choose to do it. If he knew what misery the seeking is, he would have chosen not to seek. So the seeking is something that is happening, and you have not chosen to seek. That is the basis of what I am saying.

The "one in a thousand " that Lord Krishna is speaking of, that "one" didn't choose to be the seeker—the seeking *happened*. But instead of letting it happen, letting that Power which started the seeking carry on the seeking, the ego who thinks he or she is the seeker wants to know the best way to achieve enlightenment. Why do you want enlightenment? Because you are expecting it to give you the greatest pleasure this world has given you. So I always say that the seeking begins with an illusory seeker seeking enlightenment as an object which would give him great pleasure. The seeking ends only with the total realization—unquestioned, unconditional realization—that there never was a seeker. That's when it ends.

So when does it really end? It ends with the realization—What am "I" doing? What am "I" seeking? "I" didn't choose to do any seeking. Will the seeking end in this body-mind organism? Who cares? So when the 'Who cares?" arises from the depths of your being—I don't really care a damn whether enlightenment happens or not; it's not my business; I'm not the seeker—then enlightenment is very, very close indeed.

Seeking Is a Process

RAMESH The Source started the seeking and in doing that has started the course of the ego being destroyed—which is what Ramana Maharshi said, "Your head is already in the tiger's mouth. There is no escape." Meaning, the Source has started the process of destroying the ego, and it's only the Source that can do it.

So the real point is the Source created the ego and the Source is in the process of destroying the ego in a particular body-mind organism. Therefore the ego has nothing to do with it. The ego is in the process of being destroyed. That is the main acceptance. So if the ego is in the process of being destroyed, then how can the ego seek its own destruction? And that is what's happening, isn't it? For twenty-five years the ego has been seeking its own destruction without realizing it at all. If at any time the ego had truly realized that it was seeking its own destruction, do you think it would have continued for twenty-five years?

The main point to understand is that the ego will not destroy itself. The ego *is being destroyed*. And remember Ramana Maharshi's words, "There is no escape." The seeking was started by the Source, and the seeking will proceed at its own pace according to the will of the Source. So the only thing to understand is that nothing happens unless it is God's will, the will of the Source.

ৼৼৼ

RAMESH What is the seeking about? The seeking is *not seeking the Source*, but the seeking is the removal of that which hides the Source—the sense of personal doership, the ego. You are told that "you" are to remove the ego. I ask "who" is to remove "whose" ego? Therefore I come to the conclusion that the ego which hides the Source—only that Power, or Source, which created the ego can remove it. Who created the ego? Where did the ego come from? The ego can only have come from the one Source, and the Source is in the process of destroying the ego—one in thousands. And that is the process which is happening.

GERRY *So it is a process?*

RAMESH Oh, indeed it is a process! There is a process. Certainly! In other words, enlightenment is a process. The usual concept I give is this, and whenever anybody uses a concept he has to use objects. What is a seeker doing? According to my concept a seeker is climbing a staircase. He doesn't know if there are thirty steps or 300,000 steps. All he knows is he cannot stop climbing! He didn't start the climbing. The climbing is *happening* and he keeps on climbing.

So in one particular case the final step may be the thirtieth step. The step from the twenty ninth to the thirtieth is always sudden. But there is a process and all I'm saying is, "You didn't start that process." Therefore there is no "you" to reach the thirtieth step. Twenty ninth to thirtieth is sudden. That is why they say the awakening is always sudden.

ৰৰৰ

The only way to deal with the ego is to understand what the ego is and how it has arisen: all there is is Consciousness, and it is the Consciousness which has *deliberately* identified Itself with each individual body-mind mechanism in order to perceive the manifestation in the duality of observer/observed. So, the entire functioning of the totality of manifestation, the *lila,* is an impersonal affair of evolution concerning—the process of initial identification—the identified existence covering a certain period—the mind turning inward—the beginning of the process of disidentification—and the final understanding of this very impersonal process, or enlightenment, in which Consciousness has regained its original "purity." (CC 14)

ཨཨཨ

Your statement that "this belief that I was dependent on the Unknown for this boon (being in the I Am) occasionally engendered in me the egoic fear that this bounty might be withdrawn and I would be lost." This is the core of the matter. This fear will disappear when you remember—or bring your attention to the fact—that a "you" or a "me" cannot have the bounty, that all there is is Consciousness which Itself initiated the process of identification as a separate entity. The process of identification has continued for a while, and then the mind turned inwards and the process of disidentification has started and gone a long way forward. All that now remains is to witness the "progress" of this process. Who witnesses this progress? Consciousness, of course. (CC 35)

Effort and Self-Improvement

This question of individual volition and personal effort is extremely subtle and difficult to understand. And yet it is absolutely necessary not only to understand it intellectually but to absorb it in our very being. Difficulty arises because most Masters seem to have taught predestination in theory but free will in practice! Jesus Christ affirmed that without the will of God not even a sparrow can fall, and that the very hairs on one's head are numbered. And the Koran very definitely affirms that all knowledge and power are with God and that He leads aright whom he will and leads astray whom he will. And yet both Christ and the Koran exhort men to right effort and both condemn sin. The *apparent* contradiction would easily be solved if one kept in mind the concept of spiritual evolution mentioned above. The absolute illusoriness of the individual human being—and his so-called effort—will be quickly understood by the one who is on the very brim of enlightenment, whereas someone who is much lower on the scale will more easily accept the concept of effort, determination and concentration. ... The type of human being who relies on his personal effort at one stage may, at a later stage, come to realize that such effort as is made is truly the effort of the totality of functioning and not that of any illusory individual doer.

So long as a person considers effort as his personal effort, with the purpose of achieving something, he is rejecting the all-mightiness of the Almighty. So long as a person wants something from the Almighty, he is rejecting the fact of "Thy will be done." True love of God means surrender to him, wanting nothing, not even salvation. (FT 216-217)

ৰৰৰ

RAMESH So long as there is an "Allan" wanting to be at one with God, being God cannot happen. Therefore, being God can happen only when there is no Allan wanting to be one with God. And that can only happen if it is God's will. That's it. That's the last word, Allan.

ALLAN *That's the last word. Thank you, because when you look at me ...*

RAMESH When I look at you, Allan, do you know what I feel? Deep compassion. That is what I feel. I feel deep compassion because Allan keeps on trying *to do*, which is impossible. That is why I keep on telling Allan, "So long as there is an Allan wanting to be one with God, being God cannot happen." It can only happen if it is God's will. Therefore, is there something that Allan can do? Yes! *Leave it to God*. That is the only thing you can do—leave it to God. In the meantime let life happen through this body-mind organism and merely witness what is happening.

ALLAN   *That is why I think I enjoy life more and more.*

RAMESH   Good, good.

ᵅᵅᵅ

The basis of the ultimate understanding is precisely this: that the mind turns inward not because of the initiative or efforts of any individual, but purely as a movement in Consciousness, an impersonal happening that gets misinterpreted as a personal event which is supposed to lead to some personal achievement that is labeled "enlightenment" at the higher mystical level, or at least as "peace of mind" at the more mundane level! (CC 40)

ᵅᵅᵅ

It is not often realized that there cannot be the slightest trace of intention or planning in an action that is spontaneous and natural. What is more, spontaneity and naturalness cannot be "achieved" either by trying or trying not to try! ... This may again seem to be an impossible impasse, but it is really not so. Effort (or an effort not to make an effort) is based on desire or volition, which itself is an aspect of the "me-concept" or the ego. It is the split mind* which sees the apparent impasse as such, while spontaneity is synonymous with the absence of the split mind. (EE 214)

ᵅᵅᵅ

All dualism is illusion, all action is spontaneous and all volition is an illusion. Once this is realized one ceases *to try* to be spontaneous. *Seeing the illusoriness of volition makes all*

*see Glossary

action automatically spontaneous. By the same token it must also be clear that it needs no effort as such through any disciplines or practices or devices, such as any repeated affirmations of any formulas or thoughts or words, in order to see something which is already there. The Chinese philosophy calls all effort to realize the Tao as "putting legs on a snake" because "everything is Tao." It is interesting to note that Nisargadatta Maharaj referred to such efforts in similar terms. (EE 34)

ཙཙཙ

It is extremely difficult for any ordinary man to grasp the fact that nothing more than a deep understanding, an unshakable conviction, of one's true nature is all that is necessary for the transformation to take place. It has been man's conditioning from the earliest day of his life that it is only personal effort that can bring him anything in life: even as a baby he had to cry before his hunger was satisfied. And now he is told that understanding is all that is necessary and, what is more, that any effort by a "me" could well be counterproductive. This seems incredible, quite unacceptable. ...

The wise man is convinced, beyond a shadow of a doubt, that he cannot control the results or consequences of his actions, because they form part of the total actions taking place in Totality. All that he can do is to concentrate his attention—his working mind—on the work at hand. The result is that such work—done to the best of his ability, without being hampered by the thinking, conceptualizing, worrying mind—will naturally be at its best, performed with much less physical effort, and almost no nervous strain. (LR 48-49)

ཙཙཙ

RAMESH If a person wants to improve himself, my answer to that is do whatever you want to do. What more freedom do you want?

PRATIMA *But you know that it's not really the freedom of your own will, you know it's God's will.*

RAMESH So that's why I tell him, do whatever you like. But I also tell him—having told him to do whatever he likes— what you think you like in the precise moment in the given circumstances is exactly what you are supposed to like according to God's will. But this does not prevent you from trying to do whatever you want to improve yourself. Which is what the person wants.

So I don't tell him all this is illusion, all this is *maya*. If you want to improve yourself, improve yourself. Fine. That's good.

PRATIMA *But you do say that it's maya, this idea of personal will, that you can do what you want but know that it is God's will that is occurring.*

RAMESH So my basis of this is Thy will be done. He says, "Does it mean that I have no free will?" So I say, "Has your free will prevailed every time? Have you got what you wanted every time? No. Has anything that you didn't want, not happen? Yes, it has. What is your experience?" The experience is that you know what you want doesn't always happen. Therefore I say, "What you want sometimes happens, sometimes doesn't happen, and whether it happens or not depends on God's will."

ৰৰৰ

NORMAN *A major movement today in the world is what is called the "new age movement," and one of its philosophies is to improve yourself. So I deal with my anger or whatever I had with my parents which makes my life not so happy, then I do something which changes that behavior. So how does that relate ...?*

RAMESH Wait a minute. All you have told me so far is that you do something that you think you should do. You think you should improve yourself? Then do something to improve yourself. Fine! It fits in totally with what I have said. All I'm saying is do whatever you think you should do. That is one of my basic concepts.

NORMAN *So it's unimportant whether you try to improve yourself as an individual or not.*

RAMESH "Unimportant" for "whom," Norman? It is important for Norman to improve himself, so Norman improves himself. Where is the question of its being unimportant for whom? Norman tries to improve himself because it is important to improve himself, and he tries it. My only point is, Norman, having tried to improve yourself, whether the improvement happens or not is not in your control. But it *does not prevent you from trying to do whatever you want to do* to improve yourself.

NORMAN *My own experience over time is that self improvement does not have an end in itself.*

RAMESH It never ends, does it?

NORMAN *No, and it doesn't bring about peace of mind.*

RAMESH That's the point, it doesn't bring about peace of mind. You are in competition with yourself. Isn't that what it is? The fact that you want to improve yourself means you're not happy with What-Is at that moment, and that keeps going on all the time. On the other hand, I'm not saying that this prevents you. Everything has a sense of reason in life.

ৠৠৠ

MARTIN *Can this Divine hypnosis be removed?*

RAMESH Sure. Certainly. How? Only that Power that created

the hypnosis can remove the hypnosis. The hypnotized being cannot get rid of the hypnosis. And that is what the seeking is all about. The seeking is the hypnotized being wanting to remove the hypnosis and wanting to know how he or she can do it.

MARTIN *And it's pointless trying?*

RAMESH That is correct. That is precisely what I am saying. And yet the trying is happening, is it not, Martin?

MARTIN *Yes.*

RAMESH So why is the trying happening?

MARTIN *Because Divine hypnosis is also creating the trying.*

RAMESH That is correct. That is precisely correct. That Power which has created the hypnosis is creating this effort to get rid of the hypnosis. That is why I keep saying that there is *no individual seeker seeking enlightenment.*

MARTIN *Still it feels so much as if I was real. I continue getting involved with all this and ...*

RAMESH That is itself the hypnosis. "I" am Martin; "I" am a separate being; "I" am in control of my life; "I" want to achieve enlightenment—that *is* the hypnosis. (TM 127-128)

Analysis of Actions – The Only Sadhana

RAMESH So how can identification with a name and form, which is harmless, be such a tremendous obstruction to your *being* God? The ego, as I use the concept, is not mere identification with a name and form, but identification with a name and form as a separate entity, as a *separate doer* of his or her actions. That is the real obstruction, not mere identification with a name and form—but identification with a name and form as a *separate individual doer* or as an individual doer *separate* from another *individual doer*. You see? That *separateness as a doer* is the real problem.

So how can you get rid of the idea that you are the doer of the actions which happen through this body-mind organism? My answer, my concept, is that you have to first understand intellectually, and then by personal experience come to the inevitable, unconditional acceptance that you are not an individual separate from others doing separate actions.

First comes the intellectual understanding that you are not a separate doer. Then from personal experience this concept becomes so deeply ingrained that it becomes an unconditional, totally acceptable understanding. Now how can that be?

TIM *You said one could do the practice of analyzing actions. You said that by doing this the ego could be weakened.*

RAMESH The ego starts doing it, and *in the process* the ego gets weaker.

TIM *Then you said that at some point the question is asked from the Source directly ...*

RAMESH The question *arises!* That means the ego is so weak that the ego cannot even ask that question. It could be that in certain practices the ego gets stronger and stronger. In this process which I suggest, the ego, according to my concept, will get weaker and weaker as there is greater and greater realization from personal experience that the ego is not doing anything—that the *ego cannot do* anything—the *doing happens*. Then the ego gets weaker and weaker and ultimately dies.

GARY *I have a problem when you ask us to analyze these actions. The problem is that I no longer trust my sense of either intellect or feeling to be able to determine this. I watch my mind or my feelings and at one moment I seem to feel very strongly this way, and then I discover that no, actually my feeling was very different. Everything seems so confused and muddled inside of me. I don't think it's possible to determine whether you are the doer or not the doer.*

RAMESH   Gary, I'm not saying to watch your feelings. I'm not saying watch your thoughts. All I'm saying is some action happens during the day, does it not?

GARY   *But how can I determine ...*

RAMESH   Easy! Take a simple action. You leave here and end up going to an unknown restaurant. At the end of the day, if you analyze this entire action as it happened, you will find that several thoughts came over which you had no control. What were they? "I'm hungry. I want to eat something. I don't have much money with me so I want to find a clean restaurant where I will get reasonably good food at reasonably good prices." So you ask someone, "Is there a place ..." "Sure, just around the corner."
   So what happened? There was a series of thoughts. The brain responded to those thoughts according to circumstances over which you had no control—hunger arose; you like good and clean food, due to your conditioning; you discovered you had left most of your money in your room. So the brain reacted to the existing situation and asked directions of someone, "Is there a place here where I can go?" So how much was it "your" action and how much was it a chain of circumstances and conditioning that lead you to go to that restaurant? And you come to the conclusion, "It was not 'my' action. 'I' was suddenly hungry, and 'I' was lead to a restaurant by a set of circumstances over which 'I' had no control."

GARY   *My perception is that this changes in time. That's why I say that I don't trust my senses. When something is occurring or*

*about to occur, it appears to me that I have control. When
something has already occurred, it appears to me that I had no
control. It doesn't matter what the thing is. So it's a question of
time—how I see it through time.*

RAMESH   That's why I say, "At the end of the day ..."

GARY   *Then it will always appear that I had no control.*

RAMESH   That is exactly my point.

GARY   *But if I'm looking forward it always appears that I
have control.*

RAMESH   Yes, "it always appears." You are one hundred
per cent correct. "It always *appears*" that "you" have control.

GARY   *In both cases "it appears."*

RAMESH   No. At the end of the day when you analyze it,
you come to the conclusion you had *no control*. A thought
occurred, or you heard something, a suggestion, or you
saw something. The brain reacted to what was seen or heard
or thought. You can use this analysis for *any* action, and at
the end of the day you'll find from personal experience
that it was not "your" action.
    This analyzing the action, any action, for me is the *only*
sadhana or practice you need to do. That is my concept. Do
this sadhana to the extent that is possible for you to do it—
and this depends upon God's will and the destiny of the
body-mind organism. So to the extent that it is possible for
you to do this sadhana, you come to the conclusion that no
action is really "your" action. And if this happens day after
day after day, then at some point—again, if it is the will of
God and the destiny of the body-mind organism—the
question will arise from the very depths of your being, "If
Gary doesn't do anything, who is Gary?" As Lord Buddha
said, "There is no doer thereof." That is the conclusion that

you come to from *personal* experience—if Gary doesn't do anything, who is Gary? Who am I?

This is Ramana Maharshi's question, "Who am I?" It is most important to understand that it is not the intellect which asks. If the intellect asks, then the intellect provides the answer. And the answer the intellect provides, the intellect again questions. You keep on going in circles.

But when the question *arises* from the Source, if this is the will of the Source and the destiny of the body-mind organism, then the answer comes *not* from the intellect— the answer comes from the Source. There never has been a Gary other than a name given to a body-mind organism. So there never has been any doer. Gary, the ego, doesn't exist. If Gary doesn't exist then what exists? *Only the Source.* Source is all there is.

Gary, my basic concept is that every human being is a programmed instrument or computer which the Source uses, and each human computer is unique. No two are alike because of the DNA and the conditioning each receives and over which there is no control. Together the DNA and the conditioning are what I call the programming. And what does the Source do in order to bring about an action that the Source wants? It puts in an input. What is an input? The Source sends you a thought, the brain reacts to that thought and brings out an output according to the programming. Gary says this output is "his" action. But when you analyze each action you come to the conclusion that no action is "your" action.

GARY   *But I don't know if it's impossible for somebody to gain more control over themselves.*

RAMESH   For "whom"?

GARY   *I don't know.*

RAMESH   For whom? That is the whole point, Gary. The question—Who is Gary? The answer—There is no Gary!

GARY *You say the ego doesn't exist.*

RAMESH Yes.

GARY *The ego affects the body, the body exists from a certain point of view. If the ego is worrying and upset over what it's going to do, the body may become sick. So if that which exists is affected by that which does not exist, it's illogical.*

RAMESH And that is why so long as the ego is there, it can affect the body and worry about the body being sick.

GARY *So then the ego does exist.*

RAMESH The ego exists. Now, you go out into the sun, Gary. There is a shadow. Is there a shadow or is there no shadow?

GARY *Both. Yes and no.*

RAMESH That's it! So does the ego exist? Yes and no. That is what you find out. If the ego doesn't *do* anything, the ego doesn't exist. "Gary" *exists* because the ego exists. If "Gary" doesn't *do* anything, Gary doesn't exist. So the annihilation of the ego means there is no "Gary" to say, "I am now happy. I am now unhappy."

Happiness and unhappiness exist because of the ego. So the final, total, intuited understanding and acceptance in the heart is that *there is no ego*—there never has been an ego. Happiness and unhappiness are merely something created by the ego. The ego never really exists just as a shadow never really exists—when you come into the house where is the shadow? So with this understanding that "Gary" never *does* anything, you come into the house!

GARY *I feel this ego, this sense of "me"—almost like a physical thing.*

RAMESH It is. Therefore the ego does considerable harm.

Why is Gary unhappy? Because Gary thinks "Gary" exists. Why does Gary think "Gary" exists? Because he thinks "he" *does* actions. If "Gary" doesn't *do* anything—who is Gary?

GARY *Even if I can't do anything, it seems to me that I exist.*

RAMESH Ah, yes. But what is *That* which exists without doing anything? The Source, I Am, I Am That I Am. *That* is what exists when Gary is not the doer. And when you are in the I Am there is no happiness or unhappiness—which is peace.

ཨཨཨ

JANINE *It's more difficult to analyze the action as it's happening because you have to use your working mind, and the thinking mind is there. You have to make decisions. You have to do things. It's more obvious that you are not the doer when you look at the past.*

RAMESH No, no. You misunderstand! I'm not saying you analyze your action when you're doing it. You can't. When you do something you should do it *as if* you have free will. You just do. If you have to make a decision, you make a decision *as if* you have free will. That is the whole point. Later in the day, at the end of the day, you sit back and analyze some of your actions. *Make no mistake, it is still the ego which analyzes them.* Let the ego analyze the actions at the end of the day, and find out "whose" actions. Were they "your" actions or did they originate with something over which "you" had no control, and then the brain reacted to that over which you had no control, and an event happened—which you call "your" action.

This misunderstanding, I'm glad it came up. I'm not suggesting that when an action is happening you find out whether it is your action or not. You can't do it.

JANINE *It's impossible.*

RAMESH At that moment you make a decision *as if* you had free will, *as if* it is your decision, based on facts and possible consequences. Later in the evening you analyze the action and how it happened.

That there is *no doer* is a concept, a theory. It can become truth for you *only from practical experience.* This is why you must try and analyze from your own personal experience whether it was "your" action or if it *just happened.* Otherwise, it only remains theory.

So for the theory to become actual experience, you have to find out for yourself. And gradually what will happen is, as you analyze your actions at the end of each day, you will find that as the actions are happening there will be a *witnessing* of how they are *just happening.*

Over a course of time it will *so happen that,* while doing something, you will be *aware* that you are not doing whatever because such and such a thing *just happens.* This won't occur in the beginning. But when this does begin to happen, it will be at a stage when the ego is very, very weak.

But forget about it. This too can only happen. If you keep it in mind you'll be expecting it, and that will be an obstruction. In every effort to remember, the ego is present. The ego is absent only when the *understanding* brings about the *remembering.*

This is why Ramana Maharshi says Self-realization is the easiest thing. Then he says you must practice a lot. Practice what? Asking yourself, Who am I? My point is that the question "Who am I?" *arises* from this sadhana of analysis. When you come repeatedly to the point that nothing is "my" action, day after day, then the question *just arises.* "You," the ego, don't ask the question. The question comes from the depths of your being—if there is no action that "I" do, who is this "me"? So Ramana Maharshi's question *arises* only when the theory becomes practice, and you know that actions are not "your" actions.

ৰৰৰ

MARK *From what you said about sadhana, the only sadhana that you recommend is the analysis of doership, and I would connect that with a way of lessening the grip of the ego.*

RAMESH That's right—for the ego to get weaker. My only point about most sadhanas is that there is an ego aware, all the time—"I" am doing this sadhana; "I" am making this effort; "I" must get a reward. So at the end of twenty years the honest seeker says, "I have meditated for twenty years and I have got nothing. This sadhana is useless. I must seek another sadhana. I must go to another ashram. I must go to another Guru."

My point is that most sadhanas are based on the individual doer, the seeker, the ego doing something with the expectation of getting something. Therefore you are asked to meditate. Certainly. But so long as there is a meditator expecting to get something out of the meditation, then that meditation, according to my concept, is useless. True meditation is when, by the grace of God and the destiny of the individual, gradually the "meditator" disappears into meditation so that at the end of the meditation there is no remnant of any ego doing meditation with expectation. Then meditation happens totally differently. According to my concept, only that is true meditation in which there is no individual meditator expecting to get anything out of it.

The whole purpose of this sadhana that I recommend is to get rid of the ego. Unfortunately, in most cases of sadhana meditation, the meditator is convinced into thinking that "he" will get something. The ego is made to expect something. That is the unfortunate part.

MARK *I'm just wondering. If someone practices something with the notion that "he" is doing and that "he" will get something as a result of the practice, then isn't it also possible that the practice will subvert the expectation?*

RAMESH Certainly! That's what I'm saying. In some cases,

if it is the will of God, or the Source, then gradually the meditator may become merged in the meditation—or the ego could get stronger and stronger as the expectations get stronger and there is frustration after twenty and thirty years.

MARK *I think the question in the back of my mind about all of this is the notion of judgement about other sadhanas. If one or another sadhana is practiced which ultimately leads to the enquiry Who am I? and the understanding is deepening from this questioning, then whatever sadhana was practiced was the right thing for that body-mind organism to go through.*

RAMESH I wouldn't use the word "right" or "wrong," Mark. That was the *destiny* of that body-mind organism to go through whatever process. "Right" or "wrong" I wouldn't say.

Pleasure Arising from Successful Analysis

RAMESH Having succeeded in the analysis, what is the input? The input is success in analysis. What has happened? Analysis has succeeded. The brain reacts to that event and brings about a sense of pleasure. Why not? Enjoy that pleasure.

The sense of pleasure is different from a sense of pride: "I" have done it, not many are able to do it—that is pride. But you cannot prevent the brain reacting to the successful analysis and bringing about a sense of pleasure. Let the sense of pleasure arise. And on the contrary, if your analysis had not been so successful, then a sense of failure may have arisen. That is also merely a mechanical reaction of the brain. The answer is I'll try again next time.

So the reaction of the brain to an event, a thought, or something seen or heard is a natural reaction. The personal reaction to the natural reaction is the ego. The natural reaction of the brain is not in your control.

If You Get the Message

TIM *In a way I was thinking that if you get the message from the analysis, you hang up the phone.*

RAMESH   That is exactly it! I think that is a very good metaphor. "I get the message." What's the message? Nothing happens unless it is God's will. Put the phone down! You see? What's the message? Nothing happens unless it is God's will. Put the phone down.

JOHN *We're all walking around with phones in our hands.*

RAMESH   That's the trouble—mobiles and all kinds of …

Self-Enquiry - Who Am I?

RAMESH   Does Ramana Maharshi have a basic? Yes indeed— the question "Who am I?" And when he says this, the "I" is in the Tamil language. What he means in English is not "Who am I?" but "Who is this me?" In other words, is there a "me" at all? This is my interpretation. Who is this me? Is there a "me" at all?

If and when you come to the conclusion that no action is "your" action, then the intellect doesn't ask the question— the question *arises* from the very depths of your being. If "you" have not been doing anything, if no action is "your" action, who is this "me"? Does the "me" exist? Who is this "me" about whom I've been so concerned all this life? That is Ramana Maharshi's question.

If the intellect asks the question "Who am I?" the intellect will provide an answer. Having provided the answer the intellect will produce doubts. Having produced the doubts, the intellect will produce further answers that will raise further questions and doubts. And these answers and doubts will be like a dog chasing its tail.

When you come to this conclusion from personal experience—that no action is "your" action—the intellect doesn't ask the question, the question *arises* from the very depths of your being—which is the Source, or God. It was God's will that the question arose. It was God's will that you are here listening to these concepts. It was God's will that you tried this concept of analyzing actions from personal experience. So we can hope that it will also be God's will that the answer will arise—*There never has been a "me" as the doer of any actions*. So if "you" have never been the doer of any actions, then no one else has ever been the doer of any actions either.

If doubts arise, go back to the basic—nothing happens unless it is God's will—and the doubts will collapse.

Flip-Flop and Involvement

MITRA   *We talked yesterday about flip-flop, that there were moments of calm, and there were moments when I was watching my own attachment to the involvement. Even that, it's like what can "I" do? And there was a sense of freedom with that too. It's like "I" can't do anything, so if I'm getting attached, I'm getting attached.*

RAMESH   Involvement happens—knowing that you could have done nothing about the *happening* of the involvement. Even the *happening* of the involvement was a *happening* over which you have no control. With that understanding, the involvement is accepted.

MITRA   *It's just watched.*

RAMESH   The involvement in the involvement takes place when you wish that the involvement had not happened and hope the involvement will not happen in the future. That is the involvement in the involvement. But what the understanding produces is that you have no control over the involvement, which means—all right there was involvement; there is involvement, but I could not have avoided it. That is what the understanding produces. So what the understanding leads to is that the involvement is merely *witnessed* as something which is happening without the wish that it had not happened—without the hope that it will not happen again.

MITRA *That means you just stop projecting anything into the future.*

RAMESH That is it! So you don't get involved in the involvement. "Who" doesn't get involved in the involvement? It is the ego, the sense of personal doership which is involved—"I" could have avoided the involvement; if "I" had not done this "I" wouldn't have been involved; so therefore, in order to not be involved in the future "I" must take care not to do this or that.

When you've accepted the involvement, what have you really done? Accepting the involvement means, in effect, accepting the ego. Not accepting the ego means strengthening the ego.

MITRA *The more you fight against it the more power you give it.*

RAMESH That's *exactly* the point! The ego gets its nourishment from your opposition to it. It gets its nourishment from your fighting it. But if the ego keeps on getting no nourishment, the ego gets weaker and the understanding goes deeper. That is why I say, "Don't fight the ego—accept the ego."

Many people find this difficult to accept. Most of the books, most of the masters tell you the ego is the problem, that you must kill the ego.

MITRA *And so you struggle.*

RAMESH You struggle and say, "I did this thing wrong. I

115

shouldn't have done it." So don't fight the ego, accept the ego. Why? Because you didn't create the ego. The Source has created the ego, and the Source is in the process of destroying the ego. That's why your head is in the tiger's mouth. There's no escape. There is no escape if you fight the ego. That's my point. If you keep on fighting the ego, the tiger will have its mouth open for ages and ages. You accept the ego, and the tiger will snap its jaws quickly!

ཞཞཞ

The point, of course, is that the individual is an illusion, deliverance and bondage are illusions, and the tiger's mouth is also an illusion. (CC 63)

ཞཞཞ

CHRISTIAN *The freedom which arises in the absence of personal doership, is this …?*

RAMESH But that is what you have to remember …

CHRISTIAN *No but, the first moment the absence is there, the freedom is …*

RAMESH No, no! Wait a minute. *That* is what you have to remember, what you have just said intuitively, "The freedom that *arises*," not freedom which "I" am supposed to achieve. That is the whole point. The freedom can *only* arise. It is not something Christian can achieve.

CHRISTIAN *Does it have a momentary existence? Does it fade again?*

RAMESH Until the understanding is total, certainly there is a flip-flop—"I think I've got it; I've lost it."

CHRISTIAN *But the bliss experience, the bliss experience which accompanies the sense of freedom. There is a sense of freedom from personal doership. Before there was bondage, then suddenly there is the realization there is no personal doership, and then a sense of freedom arises which is accompanied by bliss.*

RAMESH   You see, "bliss" is the word. Is a sense of freedom a sense of bliss or peace? I prefer the word "peace." And if I use the word "peace" I'll send a lot of seekers away—"If all I'm going to get is peace, I'm not concerned. I want bliss."

So the word peace will send a lot of seekers away. That's why elsewhere the word "peace" is not used very often. "Bliss" is the word! "Come to my ashram and I'll give you bliss." One thousand, two thousand, ten thousand, five hundred million dollars, so that ashram is worth five hundred million dollars, another is worth three hundred million.

ॐॐॐ

RAMESH   It so happened a millionaire having spent most of his life seeking money turned his attention to spiritual seeking. When his friends found this out, they immediately told him, "Your attachment to money is the problem. It's your greatest obstacle." One of them provided him with the number of a swami who might be able to help him. So the millionaire called the swami and asked, "What am I to do? My friends have warned me that the greatest barrier to the success of my spiritual search is *my* attachment to money." The swami immediately replied, "Don't do anything until I get there. I'm leaving right away!"

Temporarily No Ego, No Doer

ROBERT   *At some point while you were talking I felt my heart opening, and I started to weep. And then this little voice inside of me which I know very well started questioning, doubting, and criticizing, and then an understanding came that even that is an expression of Consciousness. When that came I just melted away and there was this sense that everything is just happening: everything including my struggle with my self, including my doubt of myself, and my criticizing of myself. It's just happening. And something just dropped away.*

RAMESH   What dropped away do you think, Robert? "Everything is just happening," and the total acceptance of that made what drop away, do you think?

ROBERT   *The doubting self, the me, the part of the me ...*

RAMESH   That's right, the sense of doership.

ROBERT   *That's what puts me down—"You're wrong. You're going to fail." That part just went.*

RAMESH   In fact what dropped off was "Yes, but!" That dropped off and only the "Yes" remained. So now what happens, Robert? Everything happens as used to happen before.

ROBERT   *It doesn't matter. That felt like such a burden was taken away. It doesn't matter what happens.*

RAMESH   You'd be astonished, Robert, how many have said those actual words—"It doesn't matter." You'd be amazed. At a certain point those are the words that come—It doesn't matter. What does it mean? What do you think, as a psychologist, is the significance of "It doesn't matter"?

ROBERT   *There's no egoic involvement.*

RAMESH   I would say there is no one to "whom" it can matter. What does "It does not matter" mean? It means there is no one to "whom" *it* can matter—"it" being whatever "it" is. So your coming back again and again to all these things means the weakening of what is generally known as the ego which, according to my interpretation, is the sense of personal doership—the "me." So "It does not matter" means there is no longer any "me," at least temporarily, to "whom" whatever doesn't matter.

Witnessing and Observing

RAMESH   The opposite of witnessing is observing. In the observing there is an individual observer which is the ego, the "me." When there is an "individual" observing something it is the nature of the programming of the body-mind organism, which the individual thinks he is, to judge it. So the observing by an observer is almost always accompanied by judgement. And the judgement means happiness or unhappiness. In witnessing there is no individual witnesser, therefore there is no judging.

A perfect example of witnessing is a baby, a baby who has just awakened. The baby witnesses everything and is interested. The stare of the baby is not blank, rather there is no judging. Witnessing is impersonal because there is no individual witnesser. Observing is personal and therefore there is judgement.

SALOME   *The word "involvement," is there involvement in witnessing as there is in observing?*

RAMESH   Involvement is that of the observer—by judging. Witnessing is impersonal in which there is no individual witnesser, and therefore there is no involvement. The involvement is of the individual, the ego, the "me," the thinking mind. In witnessing there is no individual.

So what is happening here and now? You think "you" are talking and "I" am listening, or "I" am talking and "you" are listening. But what is *happening* is the talking and listening are *just happening* between two body-mind organisms according to the will of God, and this is being witnessed.

WILLIAM   *You are speaking now and witnessing at the same time?*

RAMESH   That is correct.

WILLIAM   *So witnessing itself is not part of relative reality. It's an absolute thing because there is no "one" who witnesses.*

RAMESH   That is exactly the point. The happening is impersonal, the talking and listening are impersonal, and the witnessing is also impersonal.

WILLIAM   *So Ramesh as the witnesser ...*

RAMESH   Ramesh is *not* the witnesser. That is the whole point.

WILLIAM   *No, that's right, but it's difficult to phrase the question. Is there awareness of witnessing?*

RAMESH   There is impersonal awareness in witnessing. There is no "someone" witnessing. In observing there is an observer. In other words, there is a "someone" with personal awareness believing that "he" or "she" is doing the observing—and judging!

WILLIAM   *Okay. Witnessing just happens.*

RAMESH   Witnessing is Understanding-in-action.

Witnessing, Non-Witnessing, Samadhi

What witnessing does is to be disassociated from the ego while recognizing its validity as the operational element in the body-mind mechanism which must persist as a part of the psychic construct of the psychosomatic mechanism. Such an *operational element* must obviously continue to exist so long as the body continues to exist, but it is no longer confused with the *functional essence* in the body which is common to all sentient being—the impersonal Consciousness. (CC 14-15)

ৰৰৰ

VALERIA *Does thinking in terms of images stop entirely during the witnessing state?*

RAMESH   In the witnessing state there is something to witness, and what is witnessed? The images.

VALERIA *The image produces a reaction in the brain? That too?*

RAMESH   Then that reaction of the brain is also witnessed.

VALERIA *So it's not like the brain goes totally blank.*

RAMESH   Let me give you an example. You sit in the reception lounge at the Taj. You are sitting there comfortably waiting for someone. What do you see? People coming in, registering. People coming down with their luggage. People talking. Now, all that is witnessed. There is no judgement. All that is just witnessed as a picture which is really a collection of images. When does the witnessing get interrupted?

VALERIA *When you say that you like and don't like.*

RAMESH   That is one thing. It gets interrupted when suddenly you see someone coming and you say, "I think I know him." The impersonal witnessing gets obstructed by the personal recognition of someone. In the sage the witnessing being interrupted by the working mind does not lead to the involvement of the thinking mind. In the ordinary person the thinking mind may become involved, if not, then the moment you realize that it was not the person you thought it was, the personal observing may stop and the witnessing continue to happen. So sometimes witnessing happens, sometimes observing happens. Observing happens when there is judging. Let the judging happen.

VALERIA *When a judgement happens, and it is the possibility to say a judgement has happened—you witness that too.*

RAMESH That is correct. A judgement has happened because it was supposed to happen. So then that judgement gets cut off. But if you say, "I should not have judged that. I am not supposed to judge." Then it is more involvement. So if the involvement happens, then accept even the involvement, and the acceptance of the involvement at that stage gets cut off. If the involvement is not accepted then it goes on and on and on.

VALERIA *But there is no blank?*

RAMESH The blank happens this way. Again, for example, you are sitting in the reception lounge. You are physically a bit tired, mentally you have no interest in what is going on, you close your eyes and sit quietly. You are not asleep, consciousness is still there, sounds of people coming and going, smells come, but there is nothing to witness because your eyes are closed. Then that state is the non-witnessing state— consciousness is still there.

VALERIA *And a thought may come in that state or not come.*

RAMESH So if a thought comes, that thought is witnessed. From non-witnessing to witnessing of that thought and back to non-witnessing. Therefore non-witnessing to witnessing is an extremely easy movement, like the automatic changing of gears. It does not require an effort. But if that non-witnessing state is not disturbed for a while and it goes deeper, then in the deeper state you may fall asleep or it may be a state of samadhi. So witnessing and non-witnessing are easy, one to the other. And it happens more often than one would imagine.

In the non-witnessing state there is nothing to witness. Your eyes are closed. Then a thought comes and it is witnessed, and the smells are smelled, and sounds are heard. If that state goes deeper then the smells are no longer smelled, the sounds are no longer heard. And that state in which consciousness is suspended is called the state of samadhi, and to move from that state into the witnessing or observing state again may be quite a stronger shakeup.

TAMARA *In the case of a sage, witnessing is constant?*

RAMESH It is, except when the working mind is going on. When the working mind is not happening, then the state of the sage varies between witnessing and non-witnessing.

Once, the very first man who took me to the States originally wrote me a letter saying that he was going to pass through Bombay for three or four days while on a world tour and asked if he could come and see me. I said yes. So he came for a few days and stayed for three months. We had a fixed arrangement that he would come in the mornings. One day I was in the rocking chair waiting for him; the street noise was not that loud and my eyes were closed. When he came in he saw me with my eyes closed so he entered quietly and took his seat. Then something happened and I looked up. I said, "Henry, you are here." And he said, "Wait a minute. What state of mind were you in?" I replied that I hadn't thought about it. "But now that you mention it, I might call it the non-witnessing state. Now you are here, we are talking, and this conversation that is taking place is being witnessed. You go away, nothing happens, the witnessing of our conversation has not been replaced by any other manifestation to be witnessed so I sit again with my eyes closed—witnessing is not occurring, it is non-witnessing." There is really just a hairline between witnessing and non-witnessing. It is so easy—from one to the other happens spontaneously.

ৰৰৰ

RAMESH   As the witnessing and non-witnessing become more frequent what does this signify? It signifies less involvement. Less involvement means fewer thoughts, but more importantly it means less thinking. You see the difference? Fewer thoughts are not in your control. If the witnessing and non-witnessing become deeper, a thought arises, it's witnessed, and goes. But if the witnessing and non-witnessing are not at the deeper level, then that thought leads to thinking, horizontal thinking. A thought arises vertically and is prevented from leading to horizontal thinking because of the happening of witnessing. And the happening of witnessing and non-witnessing together is the Understanding-in-action.

When there is a realization that this is *happening* you cannot prevent a sense of pleasure, a sense of gratitude arising. It *arises*. You see? Until the ego is totally annihilated, a sense of gratitude arises that it is happening in "you." But this has nothing to do with "you." It has nothing to do with "your" involvement. The *arising* of a sense of gratitude *is not* involvement.

Guru

ALTA   *What's the meaning of the Guru? That's what I don't know.*

RAMESH   You know, there is a meaning of the word guru: gu-ru is remover of darkness. Darkness is ignorance. So remover of darkness means giver of knowledge.

ROBERT   *And that knowledge can be given without words.*

RAMESH   In fact, Ramana Maharshi always said that is the strongest way.

ROBERT   *The first time I saw you, before you spoke a word, you*

*were looking at me as you are looking at me now, and I received a
deep understanding of all there is is Consciousness.*

RAMESH   But it doesn't happen in every case. Ramana
Maharshi said that is the quickest way. But it can happen
only in a few cases. In most cases some talking has to
happen, some physical presence is necessary. Your having
read the books and coming here and listening, have these
made any difference, Robert?

ROBERT   *Yes.*

ཨཙཙ

The disciple is initially concerned with "acquiring"
knowledge as such at an intellectual level. The *guru* is fully
aware that there is no such thing as ignorance which could
be removed by the acquisition of knowledge. He knows
that every individual is the universal Consciousness which
has identified itself with the individual body-mind
organism, and that such identification is itself the ignorance
that the disciple talks about. The disciple *thinks* that it is
the acquisition of knowledge which will get rid of the
ignorance while the *guru knows* that ignorance is itself the
result of the positive action of identification. (DO 13)

ཨཙཙ

TAAVI   *You very beautifully presented that the ego has really
nothing to do with the truth-seeking, there is nothing the ego can
do. You were also saying it is God's grace. But it also looks like
the grace is flowing through Gurus.*

RAMESH   The Guru is merely a mechanism in phenomenality
for this to happen. For the grace to flow, the Guru is the
mechanism.

TAAVI   *Then being in the presence of a Guru or a saint is very
good for the seeking to take place.*

RAMESH   For the seeking to *progress.* When the seeking begins, the Guru is not necessary. For the seeking to progress the Guru is necessary, and whether you get a Guru or a suitable Guru will depend on the destiny of the body-mind organism. If the destiny is for a process to be long-winded, then the process will take you first to a place where rituals are done, then to some other place where something else is done, then to a third place where you are told what to do and what not to do, until gradually you move on. The understanding becomes deeper that "this cannot be what I am seeking." Or, it may be your destiny that you go to the final place directly. Some people who have come here have come after twenty years of seeking, while some others have come directly here.

TAAVI   *The seeking or the opening seems to be very natural in the presence of the Guru.*

RAMESH   That is the traditional Eastern concept. It is still a concept. It is part of the phenomenality. So the Guru's grace happening is still a part of phenomenality. It is part of the process. It is part of the Energy functioning. But the traditional Eastern way is to say that for the seeking to progress substantially, the Guru and his grace are necessary. Whether it happens or not, again depends on the destiny of each body-mind organism.

SINGH   *But even coming here, what you get is still not in your control.*

RAMESH   No! Even coming here is not in your control or what you get out of it. Coming here was in your destiny and what you get out of it is also your destiny. (TM 114-115)

ᕉᕉᕉ

[The *guru*] does his best to put into words what truly cannot be put into words. He does this for only one reason,

126

and that is he hopes that there will be perhaps a single word or a single sentence that may reveal the truth and remove the obfuscation that has appeared on the disciple's real nature. He repeatedly avers that all there is is Consciousness and that therefore the disciple, like the *guru*, cannot possibly be anything but Consciousness; further that all phenomenal objects—including the *guru* and the disciple—are nothing but the subjective Noumenon in its objective expression as the manifestation. But the realization of this truth at the intellectual level is just not sufficient because at the root of the intellectual comprehension the culprit is still there as the individual comprehender! The individual outside crust has to be shattered before the intellectual comprehension can be transformed into intuitive apprehension or apperception. And this individual crust can be shattered only by the disidentifying of the pseudo-subjectivity through a subjective experience of the sheer absence of a separate individual entity. (DO 28)

ॐॐॐ

The "doer" is indeed the obstruction, the bondage which is to be cut asunder by the word of Knowledge. It is a deep intuitive understanding in which the comprehender (the split-mind, the ego) is absent. This "happening" is not in the hands of either the individual *guru* nor the individual disciple. It can occur only at the appropriate time and place in the totality of functioning when the divine relationship between the *guru* as Consciousness and the disciple as Consciousness is ripe enough to fructify, when the *guru* and the disciple meet face to face like two mirror surfaces facing each other. (DO 29-30)

The Step Before Enlightenment

RAMESH   Manfred, what was it that was not clear before,

which now has become clear?

MANFRED *When I was here last year there was a desire for enlightenment, that if I came to see you, you could give me enlightenment.*

RAMESH In other words, you came here expecting me to give Manfred enlightenment.

MANFRED *Exactly. And then after ten days of listening I thought, "What's happening here?"*

RAMESH So last year you came here expecting "me" as an individual to give "you" as an individual enlightenment?

MANFRED *Not "you" as an individual, but you as a sage and this energy—all this would give me enlightenment.*

RAMESH So Manfred as an individual came to see another individual *with powers* to give Manfred enlightenment.

MANFRED *This was my idea, yes.*

RAMESH And then you found that this ruddy sage was just another individual who could give nobody anything.

MANFRED *This was totally clear.*

RAMESH Now, did that bring about a sense of freedom?

MANFRED *Maybe. Yes. The experience of the sense of freedom was also after Lucknow—sadhana was stopped, meditation was stopped, therapy was stopped, group was stopped, Pune was stopped.*

RAMESH   But as you just said, Manfred was still seeking enlightenment.

MANFRED   *Yes, of course! That's why existence brought me here, to see this desire. I did not know that this desire was still there. I thought, "I'll go to India again for the winter months, and I'll also stop and see Ramesh." And then after a couple of days here this desire again came up.*

RAMESH   So you've understood the basic teaching which happens here?

MANFRED   *Yes.*

RAMESH   What has this understanding done for Manfred? This understanding that Manfred cannot be enlightened.

MANFRED   *Much more freedom. All spiritual clearing has gone. Spiritual seeking has gone. Life is much simpler. Misery is gone.*

RAMESH   Yes. You know, the others listening here are impressed when you say, "The misery is gone" rather than my saying, "Your misery will go." So would you say then that the misery was in the seeking *done* by Manfred?

MANFRED   *The seeker was the misery. Manfred as the seeker was the misery. And now the seeking just happens—spontaneously.*

RAMESH   In other words, what you are saying is now there is no longer any seeker.

MANFRED   *I think so.*

RAMESH   So there is no longer any Manfred as a seeker. If the seeking continues *let it continue.*

MANFRED   *Yes!*

RAMESH   Manfred is not concerned.

MANFRED   *Yes.*

RAMESH   Yes. But you are quite right. Manfred as the seeker does not have to do anything. That happens only when Manfred comes to the undeniable and unconditional acceptance that Manfred is *not the doer*. Isn't it? That has to come first from personal experience.
   (*Speaking to another person*) This is the whole point, Stan. Stan exists because Stan does. So when Stan comes to the conclusion that Stan does nothing, then Stan doesn't exist.
   Stan exists because Stan acts. And when you come to the conclusion *from personal experience* that Stan *does not act*, then how can Stan exist? You see? Stan doesn't exist, but the body-mind exists. And through the body-mind, actions that were happening before will continue to happen strictly according to the will of God and the destiny of this body-mind organism. This is really simple, isn't it?
   That is why Ramana Maharshi said that Self-realization is the simplest thing. And I'm saying, "All you have to do is to find out from personal experience if Stan is the doer."

YOGANAND   *Ramesh, you just said that all you have to do is to find out from personal experience that you are not the doer.*

RAMESH   Wait a minute, the deepest understanding is that even this is not in your control. That is the whole basis— nothing happens unless it is the will of God.

YOGANAND   *Nothing I can do. Nothing.*

RAMESH   The most relevant point is only this: Yoganand does not act, therefore Yoganand does not exist. That is the only relevant point. If Yoganand does not act, "Who acts?" the intellect asks. Then the answer, "God acts," is merely a sop, a pacification, something given for the intellect. But it is irrelevant. This conceptual answer is irrelevant.

You see, what is Self-realization? Self-realization is the annihilation of Yoganand as the doer. When that happens the rest of it doesn't matter.

YOGANAND *I have an image of a dog chasing its tail. And when I have the realization, I see the dog stop the hunting after its tail. At one point he stops chasing.*

RAMESH No, no. The dog doesn't exist. The dog disappears because the dog chasing its tail is merely a creation of the intellect. It's an image created by the mind—so the dog disappears.

(*Speaking to another person*) Everything just happens. Robert *is not the doer*, that is the only relevant point. If Robert is not the doer, then Robert doesn't exist. What exists? Only a programmed body-mind organism that exists at the will of the Source. The Source creates body-mind organisms. The Source creates actions. And the totality of actions through the totality of manifestation is *What-Is, Now,* this *apparent* creation which is *lila*, the Divine play.

The only relevant point is that Robert *does not act.* That is the *only* relevant point. If there is total unconditional acceptance that Robert does not act, then it means at the same time that Robert does not exist—then what exists is *only the Source* doing whatever It wants to do, and there is no Robert concerned with what is happening.

So if there is someone thinking "he" has got the understanding, then the understanding is not total. The *total understanding* is that kind of understanding in which there is *no individual understander or comprehender.* The understanding that "one" may have—that he is not the doer—is the acceptance by the intellect that what Ramesh has said, what has been heard, is logical—no intellectual objection to it. This is where the intellect says, "I accept." *BUT* when it happens from personal experience, then the intellect collapses, the individual is annihilated. The individual is no longer there to observe. Then what happens is the impersonal witnessing of whatever is happening through the body-mind organism. The important thing to realize is that there is no "one" existing as the witnesser. There is only *impersonal* witnessing.

Is there a step just prior to enlightenment or Self-realization? Yes. That step is the individual not caring whether enlightenment happens or not. That is the penultimate step for the final understanding to happen. No "one" to care. Who cares? A thought will arise, "Will there ever be enlightenment in this body-mind organism?" And promptly, "Who cares?" You see? So "who" cares? There is no "who" to care!

NARAYANI *When I realize that enlightenment has nothing to do with me—I was just sitting here and thinking that it has nothing to do with me. But still I am seeking. I'm not seeking enlightenment anymore, yet I don't know what I'm seeking anymore.*

RAMESH Confused?

NARAYANI *I couldn't say it makes me more free or more happy. Yes, it gets more confused now.*

RAMESH You see, the confusion is still the ego, isn't it?

NARAYANI *Sure. I never would have thought I would lose this interest in enlightenment and still have the ego.*

RAMESH Why? Because it was the ego who wanted enlightenment as an object. So Narayani wanted enlightenment as an object which would give Narayani ...

NARAYANI *And then I understood that enlightenment is no object.*

RAMESH Nothing to get hold of, because "to get hold of"

Narayani has to be there, and enlightenment means the annihilation of Narayani. That is why I keep saying that if you had the choice, and you don't have the choice, choose to seek one-million dollars because when you get it there will be a Narayani to enjoy it. But if enlightenment happens there will be no Narayani to enjoy enlightenment.

NARAYANI *What happens to me is I realize that enlightenment is no object, and this confusion happens. There is some guilt arising, saying I'm so lucky in a way, but I feel confused. It's getting more dark, it's not getting ...*

RAMESH The point to understand here is that this reaction which you are having now is the ego getting perturbed. The ego knows that if this process continues it will no longer be there. The ego is resisting. The ego does not give way easily. The ego resists. To what extent the ego resists is the will of God and the destiny of this body-mind organism.

So what does Narayani do when she finds the ego causes confusion? What Narayani is doing now is saying, "I don't want to be confused. I am getting confused." The alternative is, "All right, there is confusion, I can do nothing about it. Let the confusion be there. Who cares?" Then the confusion will become less and less, and the ego will become weaker and weaker.

NARAYANI *So in a way it is none of "my" business whether there is confusion or not.*

RAMESH That is the point! So accept the confusion. Don't fight it!

NARAYANI *When I used to come to see you I always knew I came because I wanted enlightenment. And now this time I knew that enlightenment was not possible anymore. So there is this feeling, Why am I sitting here? It is also none of "my" business why I'm sitting here. I'm just sitting here.*

RAMESH It's just happening. So having understood that Ramesh as an individual can give *nothing* to Narayani as an individual, see what happens next time. You may not come here or you may still come here. You may still come here and wonder, knowing, "I get nothing here. Why am I here?" Let whatever happens, happen!

NARAYANI *Thank you.*

RAMESH You're welcome. Yes, Vasant?

VASANT *I just have to thank you for the increased acceptance of what you are saying.*

RAMESH So be grateful to the Source. And when I say, "Be grateful to the Source," what I'm saying is that gratitude to the Source *arises*. Let it arise.

VASANT *After this total acceptance there is no doubt.*

RAMESH And more important, Vasant, there is nothing to appear and disappear. Something which appears as an experience will disappear.

VASANT *And it's such a relief.*

RAMESH Nothing appears, nothing disappears. No experience happens, no experience disappears.

VASANT *And the war is over.*

RAMESH You see, the point is this: an experience happens and the ego says, "Ah, I am enlightened." Then the experience disappears after a week. I am unenlightened now. Terrible frustration.

VASANT *Yes. And I think this is the process, this coming and going, until it stays there.*

RAMESH   So this flip-flop comes and goes which is the confusion about which Narayani was speaking. Let that flip-flop happen. Accept it. The confusion happens. Accept the confusion. Don't fight it.

VASANT   *There was nobody there anymore who could do anything, and in that relaxation something started happening. I had been doing everything, and then the attitude happened, just forget about it.*

RAMESH   You know the story of Lao Tzu and his disciple? A disciple, his face shining with the glory of achievement, came to Lao Tzu saying, "Master, I have *got* it!" Lao Tzu placed his hands on the disciple and said, "My son, you have *not* got it." So the disciple went away dejected but completely accepting what the master had told him. Time passed and eventually the disciple returned and fell at the master's feet, "Master, it has happened." So Lao Tzu raised him up and asked what had happened. The disciple replied, "You told me that I had not got it, and I accepted it as the total truth. I had not the slightest doubt in what you said. But I also had no doubt at all that I had done everything that I could possibly do. So I just let life happen without wanting enlightenment and without wanting to do something about enlightenment. Then there was the sudden, spontaneous apperception in the heart that it had happened. There was no 'me' left wanting enlightenment, wanting anything."

Effect of the Teaching on Daily Living

RAMESH How has the understanding been affecting your daily life? Unless a teaching affects your daily life in some beneficial way, that teaching is useless.

Life Becomes Simpler, Not Easier

RAMESH Do you think because of this understanding that life will become easier—easier in the sense of fewer difficulties?

MICHAEL *It may so happen. I don't really care.*

RAMESH Yes. But if it does, it is *not* because of the teaching. That you understand?

MICHAEL *Yes.*

RAMESH Whether it becomes easier or not, you don't know. But if it does, and you and I both hope it will, it has nothing to do with the teaching.

MICHAEL *Right.*

RAMESH That would have been so whether you came here

or not. But life does become simpler. It may not become easier, life may be as hard as it used to be or as easy as it used to be, but life becomes simpler. Doesn't it? Would you say that?

MICHAEL   *Absolutely.*

RAMESH   Why would life become simpler, Michael? In what way will life become simpler? Because there is less involvement.

MICHAEL   *Exactly.*

RAMESH   Isn't that right?

MICHAEL   *There was a point where it was clearly seen that I could not possibly have the overview of all creation. Only the creator could have that overview.*

RAMESH   That is correct.

MICHAEL   *So I better leave the rudder to him.*

RAMESH   Again quite right. Which means Michael gets less and less involved in what is happening. Isn't that right?

MICHAEL   *Absolutely.*

RAMESH   Which means Michael accepts life as it happens. Michael accepts What-Is at every moment as it is, without wanting to change it. That's right, isn't it?

MICHAEL   *That's right.*

RAMESH   So life becomes simpler because there's less involvement. There is less involvement because there's more acceptance of What-Is. Really simple, isn't it? Then why do you think people find it so complicated? If this is so simple, why do you think ...?

MICHAEL *As long as there is a belief in having to do things, then it is bound to be like that.*

RAMESH Quite right.

MICHAEL *And that can be changed—only grace.*

RAMESH Again, yes. So basically the whole problem is the sense of personal doership, which is really what is meant by "ego," although various definitions are given for the ego. But by "ego" what is really meant is the sense of personal doership.

Someone rang me from Madras and she said, "Am I right in saying that you say we are all puppets?" I said, "Yes, and a very wise man called Rumi agrees with me, that we are all puppets." So she asks, "Why is it so difficult for me to accept that we are all puppets?" What do you say, Michael?

MICHAEL *Again, it is the sense of personal doership.*

RAMESH Yes. It may be possible to think in terms of all the people being puppets, but it is difficult for the "me" to imagine being one of those. And the doership is with the sense of free will, isn't it? People find it difficult to accept that they are puppets because mainly they are not prepared to accept that there is no free will.

Who Cares?

CARMEN *Ramesh, I don't understand how you can say "Who cares?" It's bothering me. There is so much suffering and people not caring what happens to each other. Sometimes it comes to the point that I can't take it anymore, and then you say, "Who cares?"*

RAMESH Now wait a minute! You don't understand the

context in which "Who cares?" is said. The context is meant for the apparent seeker who thinks "he" or "she" is doing the seeking—the seeking of God, or enlightenment, or whatever. "Who cares?" is *not* about life in phenomenality. "Who cares?" means: Who cares whether God is taking me along the path quickly or slowly—*who cares*? That's his business. This attitude has nothing to do with practical life.

To what extent does the meaning of the words "Who cares?" have to life in general? An example is that you have two people: one cares a lot and the other cares very little. The one who cares a lot will not stop caring even if he's told to stop caring for others. And the one who is not able to care for others, even if you tell him to do so, will not be able to. Why? Because each body-mind organism has a certain nature—not a nature which "he" has acquired, but which comes with the body-mind organism. One body-mind organism has been created with a deep sensitivity where the caring is part of its nature. If another body-mind organism has been created by the same Source, by the same God, with much less sensitivity, then much less caring will be its nature—over which he or she has had no control. The way one is programmed, one's natural characteristics—sensitive or insensitive—is not in the control of anybody. I'm not suggesting that the attitude in living life be "Who cares?" Rather, these two words refer to the seeker's attitude towards spiritual progress. (TM 336-337)

What the Understanding Brings

RAMESH   How will you live? You will live exactly as you have lived so far. Earlier you made decisions. Life means making decisions, so you will continue making decisions. But earlier when you made decisions—and you expected those decisions to be according to your will—you felt frustrated if those decisions turned out to be wrong. With the understanding from the teaching happening here, you will continue to make decisions and put those decisions into practice. But subsequently, the consequences of those decisions will be accepted as something over which you had no choice.

That is the only difference. Life isn't going to change for the better unless it is the destiny of this body-mind organism for it to do so. This teaching is not going to make life easier for you. If I said this, the ego would have expectations—now that I know this intellectually, maybe, and I've got the hang of the matter, my life should be easier. It won't be. If it would be, then there's a reason.

I mention this repeatedly so that people won't have expectations, and when I do I see people becoming a bit restless. So I ask what's the matter? One person said, "Ramesh, you said life may not ... In my case, at least, life has become a whole lot easier. Not only simpler because of the attitude, but a whole lot easier." So I asked him, "Just because it is easier, would you guarantee that it will be easier for others who have got the similar understanding, even intellectually?"

What happens really is this—the understanding basically comes to the importance of the working mind—that it is the working mind and not the thinking mind which is being used. The working mind is the mind that works in the Present Moment. The working mind in the Moment is only concerned with doing a job. The working mind is not interested in the consequences. Whether there will be success or not or whether there will be the money that is expected is the thinking mind. The thinking mind is the ego and the expectations. So the thinking mind always lives in the past or in the future but never in the Present Moment. The working mind dips into the past to take advantage of past experience, but doesn't project into the future. The working mind dips into the past but remains in the Present Moment. The thinking mind dips into the past and projects "its" future, and is always worried about whether what is being done now is right or wrong or could be done better.

So what this understanding does produce, even at an intellectual level, is this—the interruptions of the working mind by the thinking mind become less, even while knowing that consequences are beyond your control. And if the interruptions of the working mind by the thinking mind become less, then the working mind obviously becomes more efficient. And if the working mind becomes more efficient, your work will be more efficient. And if your work is more efficient, your rewards are also likely to be more.

A man comes here usually on Sundays. He told me, "Look Ramesh, as far as I am concerned, I'm convinced the teaching does make life easier." He's in marketing. He said that in his case what had been happening earlier was when he went and saw a prospect he would talk about whatever he was supposed to, but at the back of his mind the thinking mind was always active. Now, he says, he knows that what will happen with a prospective customer is not in his hands. What no expectations produces is a more sincere, open dialogue with the customer. He made it perfectly clear that what is happening now is that he is speaking more freely, and he said he is speaking more honestly. The point is that his openness, knowing that the future is not in his control, has somehow impressed his customers so much that they are recommending him to others. And he is doing very, very well. So he says that he cannot accept that the teaching does not make life easier.

I don't say that. But it could make life easier if the understanding of the teaching makes the thinking mind interfere less and less. To that extent the working mind works better, therefore more efficiently, and the rewards are likely to be greater. But if I say this, there is an expectation. Therefore, I rather say not to expect life to be easier, but do expect life to be simpler—no guilt, no pride, no hate, no envy. Life becomes simpler not necessarily easier. If at the same time it becomes easier, then it was your destiny for it to become easier.

The basic point that I'm making is—one, the understanding almost always has to be intellectual in the beginning and two, the understanding goes deeper from personal experience. This means investigating and analyzing your actions and trying to find out whether they are truly your actions as you have been thinking, or whether they have been *happenings* over which you have had really no control. And as the experience becomes clearer and clearer that no action was really "your" action, that it was absolutely and essentially a *happening* over which you had no control, then the ego gets weaker and weaker. And as the ego gets weaker and weaker the Understanding-in-action makes life simpler. Why simpler, because there is less pride, less guilt, less hate, less envy. Not that these won't happen, but when the involvement happens it will get cut off. Until the understanding is truly there, the involvement and its getting cut off may eventually happen almost simultaneously until even the arising of involvement stops.

ङ‍ङ‍ङ

RAMESH   As Ramana Maharshi says, "All thinking begins with the 'I' thought" which is the ego, which is the sense of personal doership. You see? But the sense of personal doership will lead to involvement. That is natural. But the important thing to understand is that if something leads to involvement all is not lost.

The involvement continues horizontally in time—there is a sudden realization that you have been involved, and then the involvement gets cut off. Does it not? In the beginning involvement may not get cut off at all, but when there is some understanding, that understanding produces the sudden realization that there has been involvement. So in a presumed scale of zero to ten, involvement may begin and get cut off at nine. As the understanding goes deeper, the sudden realization of involvement happens quicker and quicker. Thus it gets cut off at 9, 8, 7, 6 until finally when the involvement happens there is a sudden realization and the involvement gets cut off immediately. But this sudden realization is not produced by "you," it is produced by the *understanding*. That is what is to be understood. The sudden realization of involvement is not something which "you" can produce out of "your" control. It is the understanding that produces the realization. (TM 82)

ༀༀༀ

What the Buddha very clearly implies is that whatever the scriptures might say—however "holy" the scriptures—nothing should be accepted with blind belief or on trust. Reliance is to be placed only on "what our own investigations teach us." ... Invariably, if the time and place is "ripe" and appropriate, the investigations will lead to the surrender of the investigator into the teaching of impersonality, the "no-mind" state (which would naturally include the no-intellect condition) in which the "teaching" will have been apperceived without the presence of the perceiver or comprehender. (CC 45-46)

ༀༀༀ

So the understanding does have an effect, a very good effect, not only on your own physical and mental health, but on those with whom you come in contact. But there is a danger! If the understanding is not deep enough, this being considered as the wise man in the group can be very heady stuff. If the "wise man" wants to continue being the wise man, the spontaneity will be lost and it will not be long before he is found out. (CS 185)

Expectation - Importance of Doing Something

RAMESH   The trouble is expectation. That is the whole problem in life. You expect something, you don't get it, you feel frustrated. Money is really the main problem for most people. I personally think one should not lessen the importance of money. If money is no problem, 80 percent of the problems are not there. Then what remains as problems are what the mind creates out of expectation. If the expectation doesn't materialize there is frustration. So if it is possible to live without expectation, then there is no frustration.

If you meditate without expectation, then there is no problem. I'm not asking you not to meditate, but meditate without any expectation. Now what happens is you sit in meditation and all the time you expect something to happen—call it silence, call it being in oneness, or whatever. What you call it doesn't matter. But the problem arises if you meditate with an expectation.

So if there is no expectation, you live your life. Whatever happens. *Why not let life happen?* I can't say this to someone who needs money, who needs money to live, for the family. Talking about spirituality to a hungry man is like adding insult to injury. I can't tell him or her to do something and not expect money. That's why I never underestimate the importance of money. If money is not a problem, then why have any expectations? *Let life happen.*

LEGAN   *I feel I have to grow. I have to change. I have to become ...*

RAMESH   That's the whole point! *Why?*

LEGAN   *I have to become more spiritual ...*

RAMESH   Why?

LEGAN   ... *or more open, more centered or ...*

RAMESH   That's what I'm saying. So try to live your life or let life *happen* without expecting anything. The expectation happens because you're bored. The mind is empty, and the thinking mind never allows itself to be empty. The thinking mind always wants something. That's why the thinking occurs and the expectations happen. If you don't have to earn money, then do something to give the working mind a chance—do something to help people. There must be something you can do to help people around you who need help. So if boredom is your problem ...

LEGAN   *There is always this talking in this fellowship that I'm going to. There's always this talking about transformation and change, and I feel nothing is happening with me. Sometimes it's okay. Sometimes I feel I have to do something.*

RAMESH   So do it. That is exactly what I'm telling you. And do it without expecting anything. And having done something and satisfaction arises—fine. If it doesn't arise— that is also fine.

LEGAN   *Is meditating everyday helpful?*

RAMESH   Helpful for what? That's the whole problem. Meditation is helpful for what?

LEGAN   *For peace of mind.*

RAMESH   Ah! So it is peace of mind that you are looking for, isn't it? And that is the expectation.

LEGAN   *I think I'm always looking for something.*

RAMESH   Yes. That is the whole problem. So keep yourself busy doing something, and if you don't need to do anything for money, so much the better. But do something. I'm sure you can't say that there are no people who need some kind of help. There are people around you needing some kind of help. Do they not?

If you are able to help people, they are bound to say, "Thank you, I am very grateful." And that expression of gratitude from someone else does bring about a certain satisfaction. What happens when people praise you or express their gratitude? If there is expectation, then pride is the result. But if there is no expectation, then only a sense of satisfaction *arises* that someone has been helped. And if you keep on doing this for a certain length of time, then the continual sense of satisfaction is itself the peace of mind you are seeking. But if there is expectation there is no peace of mind—there is pride.

LEGAN   *I always want to change. This whole idea about enlightenment and transformation and that I have to change and that I have to feel ...*

RAMESH   You have to improve, and change, and transform yourself—that is the whole problem, isn't it? Why should you transform yourself? Why should you not accept yourself as you are? The peace of mind you are looking for will happen *only* when you *stop looking for it* and *let things happen.* Understand this! This is the very basis of the understanding—that no "one" is a Self-realized man or woman. It is most important to understand this, according to my concept. No human being can be Self-realized. In fact, so long as there is a belief that "I" have achieved Self-realization, Self-realization has *not* happened. You see?

Destiny - Funny How It Manifests

RAMESH   You know, the matter of destiny—it's funny how it happens. I have known two people, both extremely nice people, generous people—but both did nothing. One was a man I'd known since Maharaj's time. He had had a successful business selling furs, and when public attitude began to change against such things he decided it was best to sell his shop. As a result he suddenly had a great deal of money, but he also had the wrong impression that he was a very good investor. He began speculating and eventually lost it all. Then he lived on the charity of his parents. He also came here. Everyday I kept impressing on him the necessity to *do* something and not give such a free scope to the thinking mind—to put his working mind in such a position as to be engaged for at least a minimum of time. Since he was such a good salesman I finally said to him, "Take a job as a salesman." "Oh no," he replied, "I have

147

owned a shop, how could I work for someone?" So that thinking was the destiny. Regardless of what I said, he continued to do nothing. Also, he had had an unhappy childhood, and as he saw it, an unhappy life. Two or three weeks ago I had a call that he had committed suicide.

There was also a young lady who was very similar. In spite of having a talent for computers, she too used to do nothing, the thinking mind churning away, and as a result she was very often disappointed, frustrated and seriously distressed, living on dole from her country as well as the generosity of a friend and relative. She also used to come here, and I would tell her, "*Do* something. Engage in something with a view to earning your living. Don't just depend on charity. *Do* something! *Do* something and provide opportunity for the working mind rather than the thinking mind." But the question of destiny is there. Her destiny was unlike the other fellow's. She did manage to get a job, and she is working hard now. She sometimes telephones, and not long ago I asked, "How are you doing?" "Oh I'm doing so well now. I work most of the time and perhaps a little harder than I should, but I'm happy." So she's doing all right. The other committed suicide.

These are two cases where I felt maximum compassion. Each one went his or her own way depending on the destiny. All you can do is show the way, whether he or she is able to go that way depends on the destiny.

There is the story of a Zen master. He grew up living with and listening to his venerable grandfather who was also a Zen master. When he was very young he heard his grandfather often say, "Whatever is to happen will happen. Everything has a destined life." One day this boy, hurrying from here to there, knocked over a valuable and favorite vase belonging to his grandfather. The vase broke. So he went to his grandfather and said, "You know that vase you like very much?" "Yes," the old gentleman replied. "Well, it's life ended three minutes ago."

Life Does Become Simpler

FEROZE *You are taught that you are responsible for everything, but this teaching is exactly the opposite—"you" are responsible for nothing. It has happened already. I think the advantage is as you've said—it may or may not make your life easier, but at least you'll stop thinking about it.*

RAMESH That's well put—"you stop thinking about it."

FEROZE *You become very relaxed, I think.*

RAMESH Has that been your experience, Feroze?

FEROZE *Yes, in the last few weeks I would say it certainly has been more relaxed. Let it happen rather than do.*

RAMESH You have to come to the conclusion that you really have nothing to do with it. Ramana Maharshi made this clear when he was asked, "I can accept that the most important things may have been predetermined. But is a small thing predetermined? If I take this fan which I'm using and put it on the ground, do you mean even that action is predetermined?" And Ramana Maharshi said, "Certainly." You see? Every single action is predetermined—every split second.

FEROZE *From what you have said, it has to be because if this is all like a movie—you can't have a movie in parts. The whole thing has to be there. It's all over and done with.*

RAMESH That is exactly it. The movie is there.

FEROZE *So it does make things much simpler.*

Responsibility

RAMESH What does one really mean by responsibility?

149

Usually responsibility for most people depends on the consequences. When people say, "I am responsible for my actions" what is presumed is that the actions will have certain consequences for which "I" shall be held responsible.

PETER   *I was not thinking so much of society punishing or rewarding but one's own ...*

RAMESH So it's really both. Responsibility is based both on what "I" think "I" should do and on the consequences "my" actions are liable to have on others. So responsibility, as far as my own convictions are concerned, will depend on my conditioning at that moment about what is right and wrong—by and large what one calls moral standards. And how do moral standards happen? They happen over a period of time through conditioning.

PETER   *But there are different standards for people in different societies, different groups ...*

RAMESH So the basic point I would make is that there is no universal standard of morality and discipline. There may be a standard within a society if it imposes one. But the one I am *truly* concerned with is my sense of fairness and right and wrong. And if what I consider right or wrong differs from that of society, then all I can do is be true to myself. All I can do is what I think is right in the circumstances. That is the only option left to me.

PETER   *Then again this could be induced by conditioning.*

RAMESH Certainly! It *is* conditioned. One's own standards of right and wrong are part of the conditioning, which is part of the programming. Programming is DNA plus conditioning. There is a sense of right and wrong. In fact, what I say is, if there is a question Do I do this or do I do that? then my answer has always been to do whatever you think is right or wrong at that moment. Why? Because "you" are not doing it anyway. There is *no individual doer,* neither you nor anyone else.

If at that moment you think that you should do one thing as against the other, it will be based on the conditioning. And who has produced that conditioning? Have you produced it? No! That conditioning is part of God's will and the destiny of that body-mind organism. This is precisely what the Buddha is reported to have said, "Deeds are done, there is no individual doer thereof." But there *is* an individual doer *in* society. Without individual doers society will not function. So as far as society is concerned there are doers. You can't say no.

PETER   *What about punishment?*

RAMESH Actions and the consequences. It's a peculiar thing. You know that no individual exists either in this body or any other body, but you also know that society doesn't know this.

PETER   *I thought I heard you say the other day, "Do what you want." There seems to be quite a difference between doing what you want and doing what you think is right.*

RAMESH   What you like to do at any particular moment according to your sense of right or wrong is exactly what the Source wants you to think at that moment. Otherwise "you" have initiative, and my point is that there is no individual at all.

In life you cannot live without making decisions, and my answer is to make decisions *as if* you have free will. Consider all the consequences and alternatives—then come to a decision. But deep down you know that that decision could not have been different from God's will; otherwise, that decision wouldn't have happened. A decision will not happen if it is not God's will; a decision will not turn into an action unless it is God's will; and a decision will have consequences strictly accordingly to God's will. Where do "you" come in apart from the fact you make a decision *as if* you have free will? The difficulty happens with What will happen to "me"? There is no "me"! Therefore make decisions knowing deep down it is not "my" decision, it is God's will.

The responsibility is taken by the fact you act *as if* you have free will. By acting *as if* you have free will you have assumed responsibility for the consequences, but deep down you know that whatever the consequences are, they are the destiny of that body-mind organism.

According to my concept the question of responsibility is not there—BUT, all in capitals, living one's life in society you cannot ignore the sense of responsibility. Therefore, what do you do? Act as responsibly as you are programmed to do.

Cannot Avoid Pain in the Manifestation

PRATIMA   *Actually nothing ever really happens. Everything is just a manifestation of Consciousness and appears to happen.*

RAMESH   So if somebody hits you it's only an appearance?

PRATIMA   *Yes.*

RAMESH   You don't feel it? Nobody feels it? If somebody hits somebody else, doesn't the one feel the hit being made by the other?

PRATIMA   *On the relative level, yes, there is the appearance of pain, but really there is no separate individual to actually feel ...*

RAMESH   So you say there is really no separate individual, yet the individual says, "Dammit all, if somebody hits me on the face, I feel it."

PRATIMA   *So somebody hits me. That is one thing, hitting occurs. The point is to what extent do I identify that as a problem.*

RAMESH   No. To what extent is the being hit and being

hurt real or illusory?

PRATIMA *There is no problem with being hit as such. The problem only arises when the mind interprets that.*

RAMESH No. The problem arises when somebody hits me and I feel the pain.

PRATIMA *But it's only the mind's interpretation of the pain as negative that creates the problem.*

RAMESH The problem is that I feel the pain, and you are telling me it's illusory! And what is more, if I hit you, you will feel the pain. Will you not? Will you stand there and take more illusory blows?!

PRATIMA *So hitting occurs. There is no problem in that ...*

RAMESH Oh, there is a problem for the person who is being hit ...

PRATIMA *Only when the mind comes in and interprets it as a problem.*

RAMESH "Oh no! I don't care about the mind!" the person will tell you, "I feel the hurt! I feel it and you are telling me that this hurt is illusory?!"

PRATIMA *Well maybe I should rephrase it and say that everything which occurs is apparently real. Many things happen in life and they're all part of Consciousness. Maybe being hit is a wake-up call that is required to kick you out of the thinking of the mind.*

RAMESH Are you telling me, Pratima, that this would be accepted?

PRATIMA *I don't know what might be accepted or not, but the fact remains that without identification with this, knowing that the body-mind organism is not one's own ...*

RAMESH Pratima, the answer will be, "All right, I do identify, and I cannot *not* identify. I have to identify with this body, and therefore the pain I feel is real." You say that all this is illusory. My answer to all of this is that the manifestation and all of its functioning are both real and unreal just as the shadow is real in the sun and doesn't exist when you come into the house. The totality of manifestation is real in the waking state. When the sun shines in the waking state the manifestation is real. But when you are home, in deep sleep, the manifestation does not exist.

The valid question I put to you, Pratima, is this: How can you *avoid* the waking state? And the answer is you *cannot* avoid the waking state. Therefore you cannot avoid the manifestation and the *pain* in the manifestation.

Can Only Surrender to the Mystery

RAMESH Meister Eckhart put it beautifully: "All that the human being can do is wonder and marvel at the magnificence of God's creation,"—thousands and thousands of varieties of objects, each with a different programming. In other words what he says is, the Lord's creation is a mystery and all that the human object can do is surrender to the mystery and not try to solve it.

No Purpose in Listening - Just Enjoyment

RAMESH Listening again and again is not necessary with a view to trying to understand. You see? You enjoy it. It may be that what has been said is enjoyed without any purpose. Where's the purpose in listening to Beethoven's music or Mozart? Some people don't like Beethoven because he is too violent. Many prefer Mozart. Or quite a few prefer Leonard Cohen. Why do people listen again and again to Leonard Cohen's music? They like it. There's *no purpose* in listening to it.

Who Cares?

About the two questions that you ask: a) sexual distractions—"who" is distracted?! Remember Yang-Chu: "Let the ear hear what it longs to hear, the eye see what it longs to see, the nose smell what it longs to smell, the mouth speak what it wants to speak, let the body have every comfort it craves, let the mind do as it will ...." Why associate yourself, why identify with the body at all? Sometimes it may be that you are less hungry than at other times. Why think in terms of "you" being less hungry or more hungry—why not there is less hunger or more hunger? Then, when there is disassociation or disidentification with whatever happens to the body-mind mechanism—including a greater or lesser tendency towards sex—the prevailing tendencies of the body-mind are merely witnessed *without any comparing or judging*. In such witnessing, the fact that certain changes are taking place is witnessed, without even relating such changes to "my" body. This is the point: to whichever body such changes may relate, the basic point is that it is the body to which the changes relate.

This same perspective may be carried over to your other point: b) "In times of ill health, I occasionally wonder if what was started when the head went into the tiger's mouth will be allocated sufficient time to arrive at its ultimate conclusion in this particular body-mind apparatus." My very dear friend, DOES IT MATTER? It can only matter to an entity who is desirous of such a consummation, and the entity is itself the ultimate barrier to the happening of the event called enlightenment or awakening. The entity is inherent in any desire or expectation, whether the desire is for a lowly object or for a holy event like liberation. Consciousness is all there is, and whatever appears or happens is merely a movement in Consciousness. So how can there ever be any "one" to want even enlightenment? Both the tiger and the head in its mouth are concepts which disappear, merge and melt in the very Understanding. It is in this sense that Nisargadatta Maharaj used to repeat all the time, "UNDERSTANDING IS ALL." In such understanding the entity itself gets dissolved, leaving no "one" to want or expect anything. (CW 34)

ༀༀༀ

It is difficult for an ordinary person to understand and appreciate the subtle but nonetheless significant differences between enjoyment of sensual pleasures and the attachment to sensual pleasures. It is not that, after enlightenment, the body-mind organism ceases to enjoy sensual pleasures. The difference between the sage and the ordinary person, in regard to the enjoyment of sensual pleasures, is that while the ordinary person is continually in search of such pleasures, the sage does not hanker after such pleasures but enjoys them with zest when they happen in the ordinary course of life. The sage does not seek pleasure, nor does he reject it when it happens. In other words, he does not deliberately discriminate between the acceptable and the unacceptable: he is open to both in the ordinary course of daily life. When there is choice, the body-mind organism continues to choose according to the circumstances, according to its natural characteristics and tendencies, without thinking in terms of good and bad. ...

Thus the sage Ashtavakra says: "Absence of attachment (not enjoyment to be eschewed) to sense objects is liberation; passion for sense objects is bondage. Understand this fact, and then do as you please." (LR 50, 52)

ༀༀༀ

RAMESH Your real question is "How will I ever know if I have the final understanding or not?" It bothers you, doesn't it? It does bother most people. Would you like an answer? The answer, again, is very simple. When that final understanding is about to happen, the one who is so anxious to know whether the final understanding has happened or not will finally say, "Who cares?" Has the understanding happened or not? Who cares?

When that stage is reached it is almost synonymous with the understanding having happened because there is no "one" to care anymore.

CLAIRE   *I think what bothers me is that sometimes the understanding exists and then it is not there anymore and then it happens again and then it's not there anymore.*

RAMESH   The answer is let it happen. There's a flip-flop— "Sometimes I think I've got it. Sometimes I think I haven't got it." So let it happen. The involvement happens only if you say, "I don't want this flip-flop to happen." Then there is involvement. If the flip-flop happens, let it happen. How long will it happen? Who cares?

Talking About the Teaching

BRUCE   *Ramesh, when we go away from here, there may be people I would like to tell about these kind of experiences who will have difficulties with certain aspects of it. I wonder if you've found a gentle way to share this knowledge with people. How can we tell people without scaring them? I cannot just walk up to somebody and say, "You're a fiction, buddy!"*

RAMESH   The whole point is that if the talking happens, let it happen, and the effect of that talking will depend on the destiny of the hearer! People sometimes ask me, "Should I talk to them?" and my answer is, "Don't talk to them, but if talking happens, let it happen. If you want to talk to them, there is a "me" wanting to talk. But whether the talking happens or not is again not in your hands. (TM 116)

Enjoy Life

Once it is realized that the Self, the I Am, Consciousness—which is What-We-Really-Are—is the doer

157

and the witness, it will it will be seen that it is not only unnecessary to renounce our daily activities but that it is desirable to continue our normal life. We continue with the deep understanding that we (as phenomenal objects) are "being lived" in the totality of the functioning of the manifestation. The supposed doership of the "me" is nothing but an illusion. *Normal daily activities, continued without a sense of doership, are the best possible preparation for sudden enlightenment to happen.* (FT 190)

Appendix

Bhakti and Jnana

Bhakti-Jnana and Maharaj

RAMESH Someone asked Maharaj, "What is the difference between you and Ramana Maharshi?" You know what Maharaj said? "Nothing at all except that I'm slightly better dressed." He had a great sense of humor. But some of his humor was based on typical Marathi background, so many could not really appreciate it, especially the foreigners.

He said he was never interested in Advaita. He used the word *pinda*, meaning, and not literally, the "very *core* of his being." So he said the very core of his being was bhakti. He used to say that he was quite contented with doing his business during the day, and at the end of the day closing his shop, going to a temple and singing bhajans along with the others. He said he was quite contented with that. He had no interest in Advaita.

But a friend of his who had a Guru repeatedly told Maharaj that he should accompany him to see his Guru. Whenever his friend visited Bombay he would try to persuade Maharaj to go with him. Once he insisted and took him to his Guru. The tradition is that when you visit a Guru in India you take some flowers or fruits or something. Maharaj said that even the flowers he was supposed to take, his friend bought them! Such a lack of interest he had in going. But Maharaj said that on the very first day what his

159

friend's Guru said reached his heart straight away—
"Nothing exists other than the Source." Maharaj said that
this touched his heart so much.

Another story I remember Maharaj telling was that he
continued to visit this Guru whenever the Guru was in
town. At the end of the Guru's talks he would go into
another room and everyone who had attended would have
a few minutes to talk personally with him about any
questions or doubts. The Guru would call each one by name.
At the end of one of these talks the Guru went into the
other room and called each one in. Maharaj was waiting
for his name to be called, but the Guru never called him.
Ultimately the Guru came out. Maharaj said he felt so
sad, "Am I not worth even two minutes of my Guru's
time?" So Maharaj asked him, half in anger and half in
sorrow, "Don't I deserve some time with you?" And the
Guru put his hand on his shoulder and said, "What
questions can you have?" Maharaj already had the
understanding and the Guru knew it.

Ramana Maharshi used to say that bhakti and jnana are
really not two. He said in bhakti you surrender, and in jnana
you accept that the Source is the only One. Make no mistake,
seeking *always* begins with a seeker. Both the bhakta and
the jnani are involved in dualism in the beginning. In bhakti
there is surrender, until finally without a surrenderer. In
jnana there is acceptance, until finally without an acceptor.
And in jnana, understanding, the jnani accepts that the
Source is all there is, that the only thing is the
understanding.

In bhakti, the devotee surrenders, but what has he got
to surrender? What has the individual to surrender? There
is a well-known *abhanga* by Kabir. He says, "What can you
take from here? You came into the world with your fists
closed and you'll go out of this world with your palms
open." So he's saying, "What have you got to surrender?"
But there is one thing the devotee can surrender, and that
is a sense of personal doership. So what can he or she
surrender—the ego. What is there to surrender except the

false notion that he or she is the doer? So it struck me again, this morning, there are really not two—bhakti and jnana. What is the basis of what I say? "Thy will be done." This means that "my" will doesn't prevail. The only will is God's will. And by "God" I mean the Source. I do not mean a super powerful entity within or outside the manifestation.

In the *Bhagavad Gita* there is a lovely verse which says, "When the intensity of the devotion of a bhakta reaches a certain degree, I give him the receptivity to receive Knowledge." But my point is that they have always been considered as two paths leading to the same goal. Yet it struck me this morning that they are not even two.

You see, I say basically that pure Advaita is Thy will be done, and of course "Thy" does not mean an all-powerful entity that is part of or not part of the manifestation, which is where the devotee begins. But strictly the two are one if you accept Thy will be done. Then there is no "me." Why is there no "me"? You find out from personal experience that you are not the doer. No action is your action, which you find from personal experience. Then the question arises from the depths of your being—"If 'I' don't do any action, then Who am I? Is there a 'me' at all?" So you begin with devotion by saying, "Thy will be done," and you end up with saying, "I'm not the doer—if I'm not the doer, then Who am I?" This is pure Advaita. You begin with devotion and end up in Knowledge. So it struck me that they are not even two. That they are two is itself a misconception.

The basis is—if you understand from personal experience, and I keep repeating "from personal experience"—that you are not the doer. From personal experience how do you find this out? You analyze every action. As many as you can, anyway. Was it "my" action or did something lead to something which lead to something else and the action *happened*. In other words, a purely mechanical reaction of the brain happened to an input over which you have no control, according to the programming over which you had no control. And you come to the conclusion day after day—actions have been *happening*. This

161

is what Lord Buddha said, "Events happen. Deeds are done. There is no individual doer thereof."

Adi Shankara's Hymns to the Mother

BLAYNE *Ramesh, didn't the Adi Shankara, towards the end of his life, write hymns to the Mother? So there's another jnani-bhakta.*

RAMESH Wait a minute. Someone did ask me, "Look, there is one thing that I've never been able to understand, and it's been bothering me for many years. How could Shankaracharya, the very epitome of Advaita, ever write verses in praise of the Mother?" So I told him that his basic question was wrong. How could Adi Shankara write such beautiful, emotional verses about the Mother? That was the question. I said it was misconceived. Adi Shankara didn't write them. "He" didn't write them. They *happened*— because jnana and bhakti are not different.

JANE *I don't understand much conceptually about either bhakti or ...*

RAMESH You see what happens, Jane, is this—everything *just happens*. My basic point is that every human object is a programmed instrument or computer used by the Source for Its own purpose. So if the Source creates an object which the Source wants to use for bhakti that is what will happen. If the Source creates another form to be used for teaching jnana that is what will happen. You see?

JANE *Well, then I am in awe of that.*

RAMESH How do you mean? Where does the awe come in?

JANE *Because all of a sudden I realized that it's not so complicated.*

RAMESH So it's not awe, it's a mystery. You know Nick here will sing a song later in which he sings, "Surrender to the mystery." I like this very much. "Surrender to the mystery"—*not try to solve it*. Surrender to the mystery, you can't solve it. This is the way it is. The bhakti and the jnana are supposed to get together. Which way they get together, you never know.

So Adi Shankara was compelled to write those verses, those most moving verses. And those who do not understand this basic concept that the two are together and want to keep them separate want to ask this question, "Why did Adi Shankara? How could he?" And the man who asked me the question, his problem was not why but how. How could a perfectly simple, timid man kill somebody? It's as bad as that, you see. How could Adi Shankara, a Jnani, have written those verses of devotion? That was the man's problem.

That's why I say the question was misconceived. The question was misconceived because the basic understanding was forgotten. What was the basic understanding that was forgotten? *No "one" does anything; no "one" writes anything; no "one" seeks anything!* Everything *just happens!* This is why I tell you that during the process of the understanding going deeper from the intellect to the heart, there will be flip-flops, doubts will occur. If doubts occur go back to the basic, and the doubts will disappear. And what is the basic? Lord Buddha's words: "Events happen, deeds are done, there is no individual doer thereof." Nothing happens unless it is the will of God. Everything *just happens*—no "one" does anything. So if that is understood, most of the doubts will disappear.

DARA *I'm just wondering that when you say bhakti and jnana are the same, are you saying it because one will lead to the other. Why are you saying that the effect that both will have on someone ultimately leads to the same ... ?*

RAMESH No. There is the example of Adi Shankara who

really created the system of Advaita from various sources. Did the bhakti verses not get written through that body-mind organism, a Jnani, which was the epitome of Advaita? "They will always go together" is the concept—my unique concept!

Bhakti, Jnana and the Individual*

Some visitors to Maharaj, especially the foreign scholars among them, do not realize that he is not a 'learned' man in the usual sense of the word. They expect from him scholarly dissertations on various philosophical subjects. One such subject is the preference between Bhakti and Jnana as a spiritual path. When asked such a question, Maharaj laughs and says how could an almost illiterate man like himself be expected to answer it. He might also point to someone in the audience and introduce him as a scholar with a master's degree in Indian philosophy, who was surely better qualified to enlighten the visitor. He would then, perhaps quietly, ask the visitor who it is that wants this information and for what purpose. The visitor quickly looks at Maharaj to see if he was joking, but finds that he had asked the question in all seriousness: 'Who wants to know the answer?' And this question from Maharaj soon makes the visitor sense that his original query had lured him into deep waters which he had never charted before. Realizing his predicament, the Master would then make it easier for him by explaining that it is conceptualization which raises various such unnecessary issues, gets the individual trapped in its net and makes him forget the fundamental question as to 'who' is the questioner, really. Is the questioner the person he believes himself to be? Is

*Ramesh S. Balsekar, *Pointers from Nisargadatta Maharaj*, Chetana, Bombay, 1982, Appendix III, "Bhakti, Jnana and the Individual," 204-211

there at all such a thing as a 'person', an individual entity, with independent choice of action to choose a particular spiritual path?

The main point in Maharaj's teaching is that in this living-dream of life we are not the dreamed characters, which we think we are, but that we are the dreamer, and it is our mistaken identification with the dreamed character, as a separate independent entity as the 'doer', that causes the illusion of 'bondage'. By the same token, then, it cannot be the dreamed character, a mere appearance, who can be 'awakened' or 'liberated'. Indeed, awakening lies in the dissolving of this 'appearance', and liberation consists in totally annihilating the false entity with which we have been mistakenly identifying ourselves. By the same token, furthermore, awakening or liberation cannot be 'achieved' by any efforts. Who will make the efforts—a phenomenon, a mere appearance? Awakening can only happen, and it can happen only when there is the utter conviction, through intuitive apperception, that we are the subjective dreamer and not the dreamed objects which disappear with the end of the dream. To take this theme to its logical conclusion, the final query would be: How does this intuitive apperception arise or happen? But then, that is exactly the point. If the process would be within the parameters of intellectual comprehension, how could it be an 'intuitive' one? Intellect is very much necessary to understand certain fundamentals, but there is a strict limit up to which intellect can go, and thereafter, it is only when intellect gives up all efforts and acknowledges total surrender that intuition takes over.

It should be clear therefore that the identification with an imaginary, independent, separate entity must totally disappear before there can be awakening or enlightenment or liberation. The mistaken identity must first be given up before the true identity can be assumed. What is false must go, before what is true can come in. This can happen, says Maharaj, in several ways. Deep intellectual concentration of the Jnani on the source of the consciousness that we are can reach a point where duality, the basis of intellect, suddenly disappears and intuitive unicity takes over. Also, deep devotion of the Bhakta for his God can reach an intensity where, again, the duality between the Bhakta and his God suddenly disappears and there is realization that he the Bhakta and He the God are one, not two. The same result could follow through a long and arduous process of Yogic practice, or even through genuinely selfless social service. However, the final take-off point, in all cases, is the total annihilation of the mistaken individual identity. And at this final stage the miracle happens. The moment the false identity is liquidated, there is nothing left to identify with, except the totality! And this is the experience of the Jnani, the Bhakta as well as the Yogi.

Maharaj hits the nail on the head in regard to this subject of devotion and knowledge when he says that the two are so inextricably blended together that they are in effect one and the same thing. Love for self and love for God are not different. The following words, reproduced from *I Am That* revised edition, chapter 46, page 213 are truly illuminating:

That which you are, your true self, you love it, and whatever you do, you do for your own happiness. To find it, to know it, to cherish it is your basic urge. Since time immemorial you loved yourself, but not wisely. Use your body and mind wisely in the service of the self, that is all. Be true to your own self, love your self absolutely. Do not pretend that you love others as yourself. Unless you have realized them as one with yourself, you cannot love them. Don't pretend to be what you are not, don't refuse to be what you are. Your love of others is the result of self-knowledge, not its cause. Without self-realization, no virtue is genuine. When you know beyond all doubting that the same life flows through all that is, and you are that life, you will love all naturally and spontaneously.

When you realize the depth and fullness of your love for yourself, you know that every living being and the entire universe are included in your affection. But when you look at any thing as separate from you, you cannot love it for you are afraid of it. Alienation causes fear and fear deepens alienation. It is a vicious circle. Only self-realization can break it. Go for it resolutely.

The problem which Maharaj has set out so pointedly— that you cannot love anything which you consider as separate from you because then you are afraid of it, and the more you try the more difficult it becomes—is a type of problem which modern psychiatric anthropologists call the 'double-bind' type, where a person is required to do something contradictory. For example, the more you are asked to relax the more tense you become; the longer you want to hit the golf ball the more tense you become and the shorter the distance the ball travels!

A European visitor once told Maharaj: "The most important of the commandments is: 'Thou *shalt* love the Lord thy God'. But I find it most frustrating indeed, for this commandment is made difficult to obey by the addition of the words 'with *all* thy heart, and *all* thy soul, and *all* thy mind'. It is clearly meant that a mere hopefully pious act is not enough, since the added words emphasize that the love that is showed must not merely *appear* to be love, but must indeed *be* love. One may act *as if* one loved, but how was one to ensure that one did indeed *actually* love? How did one ensure spontaneity?" Maharaj's answer was simple and beautiful: Without self-realization no virtue is genuine; it is only when you arrive at the deepest conviction that the same life flows through everything, and that you are that life, that you begin to love all naturally and spontaneously. Such conviction, of course, can only come through an intuitive apperception, and Nature (Nisarga) will have its own course for this intuitive process.

In regard to the identity of the self and God, it is

interesting to note the very close similarity of teaching between the great mystics of various faiths in different ages. We are told by St. John of the Cross, in his *Canticles* that "The thread of love binds so closely God and the soul, and so unites them, that it transforms them and makes them one by love; so that, though in essence different, yet in glory and appearance the soul seems God, and God the soul." (*Canticles*, XXXI) And, further: "Let me be so transformed in Thy beauty, that, being alike in beauty, we may see ourselves both in Thy beauty; so that one beholding the other, each may see his own beauty in the other, the beauty of both being Thine only, and mine absorbed in it." (*Canticles*, XXXVI) Also the great Plotinus tells us: "If then a man sees himself become one with the One, he has in himself a likeness of the One, and if he passes out of himself as an image to its archtype, he has reached the end of his journey. This may be called the flight of the alone to the Alone." (*Enneads*, VI.9.9.11) Mystics see the relation of the self and God as something like the relation between an image and its prototype, but never more than a likeness, never represented in full, but close enough to defy expression.

Bhakti and Jnana are not really different. In the final stages, in the case of both, the identity with the individual entity does disappear, and Maharaj, in his usual direct and immediate approach, asks us to accept this true basis at once and totally reject the false one. He does not say that it is easy, but at the same time exhorts us not to keep chasing a mere shadow as the ideal. He wants us *to accept* our true stand *now*, firmly, with conviction, and let the shadow merge in the substance! If you keep chasing the shadow as the ideal, the ideal will always be receding from you, says he.

Lord Krishna points out in the *Bhagavadgita*, shloka 10, chapter 10: "I give buddhi Yoga, the Yoga of discrimination, to those ever-devout who worship Me with love, by means of which they come to Me." As the glory of God begins to dawn in the mind of the worshipper and he gets more and more involved in his love for God, Nature leads him to whatever is necessary for further progress. Maharaj says that the Guru is always there ready with his grace; all that is required is the capacity, the required kind of receptivity, to accept it. All that is necessary is sincerity and determination. Nature does the rest according to the needs and circumstances of each case.

It would be interesting to examine in this context what two of the great Indian mystics—Jnaneshvara, fundamentally a Jnani, and Tukarama, acknowledged as one of the greatest Bhaktas—have to say on the subject.

In his *Jnaneshvari* (XVIII, 1130-1183), perhaps the greatest commentary yet done on the *Bhagavadgita*, Jnaneshvara says: "By mirror of knowledge and devotion, he (the unitive mystic) is merged in Me, and has become one with Me. . . . as when a mirror is placed against a mirror, which mirror may be said to reflect what? . . . He rejoices in Me even though he has become one with Me. . . ."

In the *Jnaneshvari*, and especially in his *Amritanubhava*, we see the greatness of Jnaneshvara as a philosopher. But it is really in his Abhanga literature that we find him pouring out his heart in Bhakti. It is generally believed that Jnaneshvara, also known as Jnanadeva, being a Jnani, did not suffer the pangs of separation from God which the Bhakta suffers. But there are quite a few of his early Abhangas which show that, like Tukarama and other Bhaktas, Jnaneshvara also did pine for his beloved God. He wails that in spite of being one with God, he is not able to see Him. "I pine after Thee," says he, "as a thirsty man longs for water." Then, in frustration, he says: "Let Thy will be done, for all my supplications have been useless."

Jnaneshvara goes into a poetic flight when he describes the attainment of bliss consequent on communion with God. "As I approached God, my intellect stood motionless and as I saw Him I became Himself. . ." (Abhanga 79) Then again: "Throughout all my experience I have been overwhelmed by silence. What shall I do if I cannot speak a word? Nivritti showed me God in my heart, and I have been enjoying each day a new aspect of Him." (Abhanga 76) And further, "Filled with God, within and without, as one goes to embrace Him, one becomes identified with Him. God cannot be warded off even if one so wills. Self-hood is at an end. As desire runs after God, God hides Himself. In a moment's time, however, He shows Himself when all desires become quiescent."

Jnaneshvara symbolizes within himself a unity not only of Jnana and Bhakti but also Yoga in its various aspects. Being fully aware that it is impossible at the intellectual level to understand God's nature, or one's own true nature, he says: "The cool south wind cannot be made to drop like water from a wet piece of cloth; the fragrance of flowers cannot be tied by a string . . . the lustre of pearls cannot be made to fill a pitcher; the sky cannot be enclosed." (Abhanga 93) To him the divine appears as the unity of man and woman; Shiva and Shakti are both merged in Him. True bliss, says Jnaneshvara, is to be found only in self-vision, and describes it as follows: "He sees his own form present everywhere. He sees the reflection of form without form. *The seer vanishes, everywhere God is present.* There is neither any rising nor any setting of God. God alone *is*, and He enjoys his own happiness in His unitive experience. The invisible husband keeps awake in his bed without any partaker of it." (Abhanga 91)

According to Dr. R. D. Ranade, "Jnanadeva's philosophy preserves both the oneness and manyness of experience. His spiritual mysticism reconciles both monism and pluralism." He quotes from Macnicol the following significant words: "Not in the monism of Sankaracharya, nor in the dualism that is quite satisfied to remain two, but in the spiritual experience that transcends and includes them both, is peace to be found."

In contrast to Jnaneshvara, Tukarama's mystical career provides a typical instance of pure Bhakti. He undergoes unbelievable sufferings and anxieties until, finally and suddenly, he has God-vision, or the self-vision, which transforms his weary life into one of light, freedom and total harmony. He describes his innermost experience in lyrical verse: "The whole world has now become alit and darkness is at an end. . . It is impossible to describe the bliss of unceasing illumination. . . God and self are now lying in the same bed. . . The whole world is filled with divine music. . . Both my exterior and interior are filled with divine bliss. . ." And finally, the highest experience of the mystic: "I gave birth to myself, and came out of my own womb; all my desires are at an end and my goal is achieved. . . . all things have merged and disappeared into unicity. . . I do not see anything, and yet I see everything. I and mine have been removed from me, I talk without talking. I eat without eating. . . I do not need to be born and to die. *I am as I am. There is neither name nor form for me, and I am beyond both action and inaction.* . . Worshipping Thee becomes an impossibility as Thou art identical with all the means of worship. If I want to sing a song (of Thy praises) Thou art that song. If I sound the cymbals Thou art the cymbals."

Tukarama's Abhangas are replete with mysticism. He says that he would like his God not to be formless: "Be formless for those who want Thee so, but for me do take on a form and a name which I can love. . ." Later, however, Tukarama establishes an identity between God and the devotee: "We have now come to know Thy real nature. There is neither saint nor God. There is no seed, how can there be fruit? *Everything is an illusion.*"

We have seen both Bhakti and Jnana in action, and it is clear that they are not separate paths for 'attaining' the Ultimate. There is really no question of 'selecting' one or the other. In the mystical experience the 'individual' is totally annihilated, whatever the circumstances—that is to say, whether the take-off stage was reached through devotion, or through knowledge, or by a combination of both. The clear conclusion is that so long as the idea of a separate entity with independent doership remains, the mystical experience of the universe being an illusion can not occur. Therefore, we must accept the fact that *there never was, there never could be a separate entity either to be bound or to be liberated.*

There are millions of human beings in the world, each psyche being inclined by temperament towards that which its physical composition (the particular combination of the particular shade of each of the five elements and the three attributes of Sattva, Rajas and Tamas) indicates. If this is borne in mind, we would readily appreciate the widely differing aptitudes of people desirous of knowing their true nature. There are some psyches which, as Ramana Maharshi used to say, are like dry wood-shavings or gunpowder that need but one spark of the fire of knowledge from the lips of the Guru to set them alight. While there are others so wet that they are not capable of responding quickly even to a blazing fire. And, of course, in between these outer parameters exists the whole of world population.

In this set-up, would it not be ridiculous to talk of the difference between Bhakti and Jnana and which 'path' to 'choose'? And who is to 'choose'? When Maharaj asked the European visitor who was desirous of knowing the difference between devotion and knowledge, as to 'who' was asking the question, it was surely in this context. The entire process known as 'life', beginning with the 'birth' of a physical form and ending with its 'death', is part of the total functioning of consciousness, the relative manifesting of the Absolute Unmanifest. And the mystical experience, which takes place spontaneously in the very few cases, is part of this total functioning too. The fundamental question therefore is: Can the individual, an illusory entity, decide independently as by choice, that he wants to be 'liberated', that he must choose the method, i.e. Bhakti or Jnana, and that he would make certain effort in that direction? No, he can not. Would it not be wiser for him and, incidentally, more practical too, to accept passively *what is* as part of the total functioning, and look at whatever happens in wondrous admiration of the working of Nature? The prompt but thoughtless reaction to this suggestion often is: If everyone adopts such a 'fatalistic' attitude, no one will work or make any progress. Maharaj's immediate answer to such a reaction is: Well, try it actually and see if Nature works that way. How long can you sit still without doing anything—ten minutes? This is where the physical and mental make-up of each psychosomatic apparatus comes in—it will work according to the way it is constructed, whether in the material field or in the spiritual.

There is an extremely important, though rather subtle, aspect of this matter which is often lost sight of. It is that spiritual development in each case, depending upon the make-up of each psyche, that takes place spontaneously, and any deliberate efforts from the pseudo-entity would only create hazards and obstructions. When this fact is constantly kept in mind, one automatically keeps away from the greatest spiritual hazard i.e. the uprising of the ego. In the absence of a firm anchoring of the mind in the non-existence of an independent entity, the aspirants, whether following the path of Jnana or Bhakti, would perhaps unwittingly begin thinking of themselves as privileged persons, superior not only to those who in their view were the average misguided individuals, but also in comparison to each other. Each would consider his 'path' superior to the other's. But in reality there is no difference between Jnana and Bhakti. The aspirant on the path of Jnana, while listening to the words of his Jnani Guru, finds his eyes misting and his consciousness almost in abeyance when the arrow of the Guru's words hits the target. So is the Bhakta totally lost in the devotional song and dance of the Guru and his fellow disciples. Can there be any real difference between the two?

We seem to have arrived at a working formula on the subject. *What is the individual to do?* The only thing one can do is always to keep in mind the fact that an independent entity cannot exist, and also the fact that the entire manifestation is the functioning of consciousness in which each one of us has one's allotted role to play and, finally, to accept whatever happens within that total functioning with a sense of wondrous admiration. The one thing that remains thereafter is not any 'practising' as a deliberate effort, but merely to let our true understanding deeply impregnate our very being, passively and patiently, so that all illusions and obstructions gradually fall off by themselves.

Key To Quoted Works

Published works by Ramesh that are quoted have the following two-letter designations. Transcribed satsang material is not referenced.

CC   *Consciousness To Consciousness*
      (second edition)
CS   *Consciousness Speaks*
CW   *Consciousness Writes* (privately published)
      [Note: there is an edition published by Zen
      Publications]
DO   *A Duet of One*
EE   *Explorations Into The Eternal*
ET   *Experiencing The Teaching*
FT   *The Final Truth*
LR   *Letters From Ramesh*
      (privately published)
TM   *Your Head In The Tiger's Mouth*

Glossary Of Concepts*

The created object *cannot*
possibly *know* the Creator Subjectivity

abhanga
Spontaneous outpouring of a keen devotee revealing the very core of Advaita; for centuries *abhangas* have served as succinct and direct pointers to Consciousness; often put to music and sung as a bhajan; *see* Advaita, bhajan

Adi Shankara
see Shankara

Advaita
Nonduality, *a* + *dvaita*, not dual; all there is is Consciousness, and all phenomenal existence is illusion, *maya*; the most important branch of Vedanta philosophy; *see* Consciousness, *maya*, Vedanta

ahankara
Ego; *see* ego

Ananda
Peace; *see Sat-Chit-Ananda*

arises, arising
see happens, happening

Aum
The sound of these three letters, now generally

---

*Ramesh S. Balsekar, *Your Head In The Tiger's Mouth*, Zen Publications, Bombay, 1998, Glossary Of Concepts, 401-421. [Note: updated for *Who Cares?!*]

considered a word, denotes Consciousness, Brahman; believed to be the most sacred mantra; the letter A stands for the world of the senses, the letter U stands for the subconscious mind, and M stands for *Prajna*, the state beyond mind; usually written as Om; *see* mantra

avatar

Incarnation; descent of a deity (i.e., Vishnu descending as Rama and Krishna)

awakening

see enlightenment

Bhagavad Gita

Literally the song of God; part of the *Mahabharata* in which a dialogue takes place between Lord Krishna and the warrior Arjuna just prior to the decisive battle

bhajan

Devotional practice, prayer; generally used to mean devotional words set to music and sung as a form of worship

bhakta

Devotee; often used to refer to a seeker following the path of bhakti, as distinguished from that of jnana, however, bhakti and jnana are not two; *see* jnana, seeker

bhakti

Devotion and surrendering as a path to enlightenment, however, bhakti and jnana are not two; *see* enlightenment, bhakta, seeking

bhoga, (bhogi)

Experience(er) of sensual reactions

body-mind organism

Mechanism through which life and living happen; part of the totality of manifestation of Consciousness in which the ego ignorantly assumes the role of apparent doership and hence separateness; the body-mind organism, not the ego, has a destiny; *see* destiny, ego, manifestation

Brahma

One of the gods of the Hindu trinity, *see* trinity

brahmachari (m), ***brahmacharini*** (f)

One who leads the life of *brahmacharya*

brahmacharya
Living in Brahman; enquiry into Brahman, or Consciousness; traditionally, although mistakenly, it has come to mean celibacy

Brahman
Consciousness, Source, Totality, the Absolute; a concept for the ultimate Reality in Hinduism; *see* Consciousness

brain
In the body-mind organism the mechanism which spontaneously *reacts* according to its programming, without *judging* the thoughts received or the input of the senses; *see* body-mind organism, programming, thinking mind, thought, working mind

Chit
Consciousness; *see* Sat-Chit-Ananda

concept
Anything that can be agreed with or disagreed with; any thought, idea, experience, name, thing, entity, or no-thing

conditioning
All the experiences of a body-mind organism—over which it has no control—of its entire environment (parents, family, society, culture, geography, school, etc.) which form the patterns and responses of the brain; *see* body-mind organism, brain, ego, programming

Consciousness
All there is is Consciousness; the basic perennial principle behind all religions and spiritual paths before corruption by interpretations and formal rituals; It has no aspects or qualities; It *cannot* be conceptualised but is given a name so It can be indicated or pointed to; It is *referred* to by many names—God, I-I, Noumenon, Potential, Reality, Self, Source, Subjectivity, Tao, That, Totality, Truth, Unicity, etc.; unmanifested It is referred to as being "at rest" or transcendent, manifested It is referred to as being "in action" or immanent; Consciousness not aware of Itself becomes aware of Itself as I Am; *see* concept, I Am

consciousness

All there is is Consciousness, but lower-case c indicates Consciousness identified with a body-mind organism; *see* Consciousness-in-action, ego, I Am

Consciousness-at-rest

Consciousness unmanifested, transcendent; Potential unpotentialized; *see* Consciousness

Consciousness-in-action

Consciousness manifest, immanent; Consciousness reflected within Itself as the totality of manifestation; *see* Consciousness

darshan

Seeing, meeting

death

Death is only of the body-mind organism and ego, the sense of a separate and personal identity; at death the energies of Consciousness-in-action which had assumed personal identity in life as a body-mind organism return to the pool of Consciousness; *see* ego, body-mind organism, pool of Consciousness

deep sleep

The state in which the I Am is present without any aspect of manifestation, which also means no personal or ego identity; temporary death; *see* ego, I Am

destiny

All there is is Consciousness; there is no doer and no free will—all is the impersonal functioning of Consciousness, or God's will; life is a movie which is produced, written, cast, directed, acted, and watched by Consciousness on the screen of Consciousness; the body-mind organism has a destiny, the ego has no destiny; the key, which is not in the control of the *apparent* individual, is the complete acceptance of What-Is; decisions have to be made, so live life *as if* there is free will, making decisions with your standards of ethics, morality, and responsibility, and whatever the decision is will be God's will; *see* Consciousness, What-Is

dharma

The programming of the body-mind organism; inherent property; natural characteristic; in Hinduism the firm code of conduct and duty of the individual; *see* body-mind organism, programming

dhyana

Meditation; *see* meditation

Divine hypnosis

Mechanism through which Consciousness expresses a sense of personal doership in a body-mind organism; *see* doer, *maya*

doer, doership

For the impersonal functioning of Consciousness, or God, through manifestation or life as we know it to happen, the basis of life is the sense of personal doership; Divine hypnosis creating the illusory ego's belief that it has free will; the sense of doership is unhappiness; spiritual seeking is the process of getting rid of personal doership; *see* ego, free will

dualism

The ego functions in dualism, which is the mental split between the "me" and the "other"; the mind, ego, does not accept the functioning of duality, the interdependence of opposites, but creates a conflict between the two members of a pair of opposites by wanting one in exclusion of the other (good-bad, beautiful-ugly, easy-difficult); what is absent in enlightenment is dualism; *see* duality

duality

Pairs of interconnected opposites, neither of which can exist without the other (i.e., happy-unhappy, positive-negative, light-dark); one of the essential mechanisms by which the totality of manifestation functions; when the ego becomes involved, duality becomes dualism; *see* ego, dualism, functioning

dvaita

Two, dual; *see* Advaita

education

Accumulation of concepts; to one degree or another a necessity for living in society; "learned ignorance"; *see* concept

ego

The sense of personal doership; Consciousness-in-action assuming identification as a "doer," thinking mind, with a separate name and form; the user of the word ego must know that the primary meaning is the mistaken belief of being a "doer," because a sage continues to have name and form, a body-mind organism, but *without* a sense of being a "doer"; *see* Consciousness-in- action, body-mind organism, Divine hypnosis, thinking mind

enlightenment

The spontaneous impersonal event at the end of the process of seeking in which there is the spontaneous, intuited, total understanding in the heart that there is no doer and never was a doer or seeker—the ego, the "me," is completely annihilated; *see* doer, ego, seeker, seeking

free will

All there is is Consciousness, there is absolutely no free will; everything is God's will, the impersonal functioning of Consciousness, manifesting as destiny, individual or otherwise; decisions have to be made, so one makes them *as if* there is free will—the result is God's will; *see* destiny

functioning

Consciousness is all there is. There is no doer, no seeker, no decision maker, no lover, *but* there is *doing, seeking, deciding, loving;* functioning is the impersonal movement of Consciousness-in-action that gives the manifestation the *appearance of being real.* For example, the ego, sense of personal doership, interprets as "its functioning" that which is always and can only be the impersonal "functioning" of Consciousness through a body-mind organism; *see* manifestation

Gayatri

A verse from the Vedas used as a mantra

God

Consciousness, Source; not an entity; not personal; *see* Consciousness

grace

The totality of manifestation is grace; the prevalent misunderstanding is the ego's involvement in dualism and thus not accepting What-Is as grace; the ego refers to what is difficult as God's will and what is special and beneficial as God's grace; *see* dualism, involvement, What-Is

gunas

Attributes, qualities; the three primary attributes of the totality of manifestation are *sattva*, *rajas*, and *tamas*; *see* each attribute

Guru

Spiritual preceptor; the living expression of the Sadguru that has no sense of personal doership and through which a seeker may experience his or her True Nature; *see* Sadguru

Guru Purnima

The full moon (*purnima*) day in July-August on which the disciple renews his or her dedication to the Guru

happens, happening

This indicates an occurrence without any doer doing anything; the impersonal functioning of Consciousness-in-action; "happens" is spontaneous and without intention or volition, although there usually appears to be a chain of events, cause and effect, which leads to something that *just happens*. The meaning of this word is best conveyed by two examples:

- "The teaching *happens* through Ramesh." In other words, there is no "one" who does anything. It, the teaching, *happens*.

- "There is no seeker. The seeking is just *happening*."

heart

The understanding becomes complete when it is spontaneously intuited in the heart; in the heart there is intuited understanding, there is no "me" to understand anything; *see* intellect

horizontal

The involvement of the thinking mind; *see* involvement, thinking mind

I Am

The initial manifestation of impersonal Consciousness in the awareness I Am, other than which nothing exists; the only Truth since It cannot be disputed—thus It is not a concept unless conceived by subsequent thinking based on the feeling of a personal identity; the interval between two thoughts, between two expectations; *see* Consciousness, I-I

I-I

Ramana Maharshi's reference to Consciousness, Source, Totality; I-I and I Am are not two, I-I becomes I Am in manifestation, I-I becomes aware of Itself as I Am; *see* Consciousness, I Am

intellect

The understanding usually begins in the thinking mind—for the understanding to be complete and final it must be intuited in the heart; a well developed and concentrated intellect is necessary for the process of seeking on the path of jnana and dealing competently with the manifestation; *see* heart, thinking mind

involvement

The nonacceptance of What-Is; the cause of suffering; the ego's mistaken belief that it has free will and consequently in a continuous state of being judgmental, deciding, and being concerned about consequences; this concept correlates to the concept of attachment in Buddhism; *see* ego, free will, thinking mind, What-Is

Ishwara

In Hinduism Consciousness-in-action deified as in charge of the Universe

Janaka

King Janaka is the "superbly ripe disciple" of his Guru, Ashtavakra, in the *Ashtavakra Gita* translated by Ramesh in his book *A Duet of One japa*

Repetition of the name or names of God, literally "muttering"; constant, it repels all other thoughts; vocal, it becomes mental and is the same as meditation

jiva

The individual, identified consciousness; *see* ego

jnana

Understanding, especially the total, spontaneous, intuited understanding in the heart; understanding and acceptance as a path to enlightenment; jnana and bhakti are not two, however, bhakti becomes jnana prior to enlightenment (even if it is a split second before); *see* bhakti, jnani

Jnaneshwar

A great Indian sage who was fundamentally a jnani, but from the *abhanga*s he wrote it can be seen that he symbolises within himself a unity not only of jnana and bhakti but also yoga in its various aspects; the *Jnaneshwar* classic *Anubhavamrita*, or *Amritanubhava*, is translated by Ramesh in his book *Experience of Immortality*

jnani

One who understands; currently used to refer to a seeker following the path of jnana as distinguished from that of bhakti, however, jnana and bhakti are not two; *see* bhakti, jnana, seeker

karma

Consciousness manifesting as action which is the principle of cause and effect; one of the fundamental, functioning mechanisms of the totality of manifestation for life to happen as we know it; a cause, action, leads to an effect which in turn becomes a cause leading to another effect, and so on; *see* functioning, manifestation

kriya

Spontaneous movement(s) or reaction(s) of the body-mind organism caused by movement of the *kundalini* energy

kundalini

In Hinduism, an aspect of the feminine creative energy

symbolised as a serpent lying dormant at the base of the spine until aroused; a potentially dangerous practice; the arising of the *kundalini* is not a prerequisite for enlightenment; *see* enlightenment

liberation

see enlightenment

lila

In Hinduism the play or game of God; the totality of manifestation looked upon as the Divine play; *see* destiny, manifestation

maha

Great; usually a prefix to a noun making it great or superior

Maheshwara

see Shiva

manifestation

Consciousness unmanifest reflected within Itself as the totality of What-Is; *see* Consciousness, *maya*

mantra

Instrument of thought; hymn, incantation; ideal or sacred sounds of certain syllables or words, the repetition of which may lead to material or spiritual benefits—if it is the destiny of the body-mind organism repeating them

maya

Illusion; delusion; the veiling power which conceals Consciousness unmanifest from Consciousness *reflected* within Itself as the totality of manifestation; the identification with the body-mind organism as a separate individual and doer; *see* Consciousness, doer, manifestation

"me"

see ego

meditation

When meditation happens you know it because there is a feeling of emptiness; some body-mind organisms are not programmed to meditate so there is no question of right or wrong about meditating; not a must but if it happens it is good; involves a doer if there is effort and expectation;

for the beginner, meditate on the fact that "you" have no free will; that meditation is true meditation in which there is no doer of the meditation; *see* doer, free will, sadhana

mind

Consciousness-in-action as a *functioning* of thoughts received and subsequent thinking (the *physical mechanism* for receiving and spontaneously reacting to thought is the brain); the processing of thoughts received takes place in either of the two aspects of mind—working mind or thinking mind—in the latter the ego is involved; the destruction of the thinking mind, which can only be God's will, is the intuited understanding in the heart that there is no doer, no separation from Consciousness, which is the *essence* of mind; *see* brain, thinking mind, thought, working mind

moksha

Liberation; *see* enlightenment

nirguna

Without form or attributes

Nisargadatta Maharaj

Ramesh's final Guru; his teachings can be found in Ramesh's book *Pointers from Nisargadatta Maharaj*

Noumenon

Consciousness unmanifest; there is no plural for this word; *see* Consciousness

Now

see What-Is

observing

In observing there is an observer, an ego; *see* ego, witnessing

Om

see **Aum**

play

see lila

pool of Consciousness

A concept referring to energies which may or may not have been manifested as matter or non-matter in general or specifically as a body-mind organism; at the dissolution of matter or the death of a body-mind organism the energies return to the pool of Consciousness and may or may not again appear manifested; *see* rebirth

pradakshina

Devotional circumambulation of a sacred object or holy place

Prajna

Unselfconscious Knowledge; *see* Consciousness

predestination

see destiny

Present Moment

see What-Is

programming

Genes plus conditioning, over which the body mind organism has no control, determines the way the brain reacts to all input; the mechanism by which the destiny of a body-mind organism is carried out; *see* body-mind organism, brain, conditioning, destiny, ego

psychosomatic apparatus

see body-mind organism

puja

Ceremonial or ritual worship

rajas

Motivity, activity, energy; one of the three *gunas*; refers to the activating aspect of manifestation without which the other constituents could not manifest their inherent qualities; *see gunas*

Ramakrishna

The great Bengali bhakta sage who lived at Dakshineshwar in Calcutta in the nineteenth century

Ramana Maharshi

The great jnani sage of Arunachala who lived all of his adult life in Tiruvannamalai, Tamil Nadu; Ramesh said in satsang, "To me, in phenomenality, there is nothing higher than Ramana Maharshi."

realisation

see enlightenment

rebirth

There is no individual so there can be no rebirth of that which does not exist; there are past births and from them, at the deaths of the body-mind organisms, the functioning energies return to the pool of Consciousness to perhaps again, in another combination, pass into a future body mind organism—thus there are apparent past-life memories by some body-mind organisms of prior births; eventually, energies of such refinement may come together in a body-mind organism in which the process of seeking ends in enlightenment; *see* enlightenment, body-mind organism, ego, pool of Consciousness

rishi

Ancient sage

Sadguru

The Guru within you—the Self, or Consciousness

sadhaka

A seeker who practices sadhana; *see* sadhana

sadhana

Spiritual practice or practices involving a doer (seeker) which *may* precede the goal of enlightenment; the goal may or may not happen depending upon the destiny of the seeker; if sadhana happens, let it happen; traditional sadhanas are meditation, yoga, and selfless service (*seva*); a body-mind organism may be programmed to do one type of sadhana and not another; Ramesh's only recommended sadhana is analysis or investigation of actions; *see* Index for "analysis of actions"

sage

A body-mind organism in which enlightenment has happened; a sage may be regarded as saintly, but a saint is not necessarily a sage; *see* enlightenment

saguna

With form and attributes

saint

see sage

samadhi

A state of meditation beyond mind; absorption in the Self

189

Sat

Existence, Being; *see Sat-Chit-Ananda*

Sat-Chit-Ananda

Being-Consciousness-Peace; in Hinduism the three "attributes" of attributeless Brahman, or the Source; *see* Consciousness

satsang

Association with the Truth—or one who has the Understanding

sattva

Being, existence, reality· one of the three *gunas*; it stands for equilibrium and manifests itself as light; *see gunas*

seeker

The ego mistakenly believing it is a doer and separate and thus a seeker seeking something sought; *see* ego, seeking

seeking

One of the innumerable and *impersonal* processes of Consciousness manifest; "from the first moment a baby seeks its mother's breast intuitively, life is nothing but seeking," regardless of what it is for; that there is no doer and no thing done and thus no seeker and no thing sought is the final understanding prior to the end of the process of seeking; *see* enlightenment, ego

Self-realisation

see enlightenment

seva

Selfless service, service without any expectations

shakti

Power, energy, capacity; in the totality of manifestation of Consciousness, or Shiva, within Itself, *shakti* is portrayed as the female energy of duality, Shiva-Shakti; she is deified, often with the name of Parvati, as the wife of Shiva; *see* Shiva

Shankara

Also called Adi Shankara and Shankaracharya; an eighth century philosopher and reformer of Hinduism who

established the school of unqualified Advaita Vedanta
Shiva
Consciousness unmanifest; when manifest he is portrayed as the male energy of duality, Shiva-Shakti; he is deified as the husband of Shakti; one of the gods of the Hindu trinity; *see shakti*, trinity
siddha
Refers to a perfected sage (but with the understanding that *siddhis* are not necessary or prerequisite to enlightenment); often used to refer to one who has psychic powers or "gifts"
siddhi
The final "accomplishment" or enlightenment; has come to mean psychic power (which is often an obstruction to enlightenment because the ego becomes involved)
silence
Noninvolvement or nonidentification with thought(s); a sage is always in silence; silence between the Guru and the disciple is heart-to-heart speech; *see* involvement, sage
Source
see Consciousness
split mind
see whole mind
tamas
Darkness, inertia, passivity, restraint; one of the three *gunas*; *see gunas*
Tao
see Consciousness
thinking
The functioning of thoughts received by the brain which can either be uninvolved as in the working mind or involved as in the thinking mind; *see* brain, functioning, thinking mind, thought, working mind
thinking mind
The horizontal aspect of mind in which the ego is involved with thinking and concerned with *future consequences* for itself—i.e., worry or anxiety for whether

an action will be beneficial or harmful, or for what others may think; not accepting What-Is; both the thinking mind and the working mind judge, but the thinking mind is also judgmental; both the thinking mind and the working mind are involved in what is being done, but the thinking mind thinks "'I' am doing it" and is personally concerned with future consequences; *see* horizontal, thought, What-Is, working mind

thought

Thought does not originate in the body-mind organism, it comes from outside and a split-second later the brain spontaneously reacts according to its programming; a thought is an input which brings about an output which leads to causation; both thought and the reaction(s) of the brain are vertical, in the Present Moment—if the ego gets involved (the thinking mind) then there is horizontal involvement in time; *see* brain, Present Moment, programming, thinking mind, working mind

Tiruvannamalai

The town in the state of Tamil Nadu in south-east India where Ramana Maharshi spent his entire adult life at the foot of the holy hill Arunachala

Totality

see Consciousness

trinity

The Hindu trinity is Brahma the creator, Vishnu the preserver, and Shiva—or Maheshwara—the destroyer

Tukaram

One of India's greatest bhakta sages who, following enlightenment, wrote devotionally as a pure jnani; wrote *abhangas* which have been set to music and are sung as bhajans

understanding, total

The spontaneous, intuited understanding in the heart that there is no doer; *see* enlightenment, doer

Unicity

see Consciousness

Upanishads

Concerned with pure knowledge, these ancient philosophical texts are much later than the original Vedas; the texts from which all Vedanta philosophy originates; *see* Vedanta, Vedas

Vedanta

Literally, the end of the Vedas, the culmination of knowledge; philosophy based upon the Upanishads; Advaita Vedanta is the most well-known branch of Vedanta; *see* dvaita, Upanishads

Vedas

The most ancient of the sacred literature of Hinduism; they start out as mythical and ritual texts and culminate in the pure philosophy of Vedanta; *see* Vedanta

vertical

Being in the Present Moment, or What-Is; cuts off horizontal involvement; only the working mind is functioning; *see* horizontal, What-Is, working mind

Vishnu

One of the gods of the Hindu trinity; *see* trinity

What-Is

Outside of space-time It neither is nor is not—past, present, and future and all of their apparent contents are *spontaneously* happening *simultaneously*; this state/non-state is also referred to as Present Moment and Here and Now; cannot be "experienced" by the ego

whole mind

Consciousness-in-action, I Am, is whole mind and becomes split or divided when identified with the body-mind organism as a "me"; (Note: whole mind/split mind and working mind/thinking mind are two different concepts and cannot be compared or interchanged); *see* split mind

witnessing

In witnessing there is no "one" doing the witnessing, there is no ego present; *see* ego, observing

working mind

The vertical aspect of mind which is only in the Present Moment—the ego is not present with its concerns for future consequences; the working mind uses judgement and consideration of consequence to do the best it can with the knowledge it has for a task, but the judging and consideration of consequence are *in the Present Moment,* or What-Is, and there is *no* personal concern for *future* consequences; while the working mind is functioning there is little or no sense of time and place unless such consideration is part of the task at hand; in the sage there is *only* the working mind, there is *no* thinking mind; (Note: working mind/thinking mind and whole mind/split mind are two different concepts and cannot be compared or interchanged); *see* thinking mind, vertical, What-Is

Index

(also see Glossary)

More From Advaita Press

A Duet of One by Ramesh S. Balsekar
Here Ramesh uses the Ashtavakra Gita as a vehicle for an illuminating look at the nature of duality and dualism.
Softcover 224 Pages $16.00

Who Cares?! by Ramesh S. Balsekar

This is the boook we recommend to those asking for a book that will describe the essence of Ramesh's teaching. Ramesh's ability to cut through to the simple heart of complex ideas is a joy to experience. Softcover 220 Pages $16.00

Acceptance of What IS by Wayne Liquorman
The latest look at Advaita through the eyes of the most unlikely of Sages. Wayne's expression of his spiritual understanding is at once irreverent and profound. We laugh, sometimes joyously, sometimes uncomfortably but always with the recognition that we are in the presence of a Master. Softcover 304 Pages $16.00

Your Head In The Tiger's Mouth by Ramesh S. Balsekar

A superb overview of the Teaching. Transcribed portions of talks Ramesh gave in his home in Bombay during 1996 and 1997.
Softcover 472 Pages $24.00

A Net Of Jewels by Ramesh S. Balsekar
A handsome gift volume of jewels of Advaita, selections from Ramesh's writings presented in the format of twice daily meditations. Hardcover 384 Pages $25.00

Consciousness Speaks by Ramesh S. Balsekar

Ramesh's most accessible and easy to understand book. Recommended both for the newcomer to Advaita and the more knowledgeable student of the subject.
Softcover 392 Pages $19.00

Ripples by Ramesh S. Balsekar
A brief and concise introduction to Ramesh's Teaching. Perfect to give to friends. Softcover 44 Pages $6.00

SEE NEXT PAGE FOR ORDERING DETAILS

www.advaita.org

NO WAY *for the spiritually advanced* by Ram Tzu

 No Way is a unique blending of wit, satire and profound spiritual insight. One minute we are howling with unconstrained laughter, the next we are squirming in self-conscious recognition as Ram Tzu holds up a perfect mirror and then gleefully points out that we aren't wearing any clothes.
Softcover - 112 Pages $13.00
Also available on Audio Cassette $15.00

===============

If unavailable at your bookstore, these titles and many others may be ordered directly from the Advaita Press Store at **www.advaita.org**

OR

Send check, money order or Visa/Mastercard or American Express number (include expiration date and billing zip code) for the indicated amount plus shipping as noted below to:

Advaita Press
P.O. Box 3479 DOI2
Redondo Beach, CA 90277
USA

Shipping & Handling:

In U.S. :

    Surface mail: First book $4.00. Add $1.00 each additional.
    Airmail: First book $6.00. Add $1.00 each additional book.

Outside U.S.Å.:

    Canada Airmsil: First Book $8.00. Add $4.00 each additional.
    International Airmail: $12.00 per book.
    International Surface mail: $6.00 per book

Payment in U.S. dollars via credit card, check or money order payable on a U.S. bank. No Eurochecks please.

www.advaita.org

CPSIA information can be obtained at www.ICGtesting.com
Printed in the USA
LVOW11s1547010614

388115LV00001B/183/P